How to Have a Baby and Not Lose Your Shit

Kirsty Smith

DARK
RIVER

An imprint of Bennion Kearny

Published in 2015 by Dark River, an imprint of Bennion Kearny Limited.

Copyright © Dark River

ISBN: 978-1-911121-04-6

Published by Dark River, an imprint of Bennion Kearny Limited
6 Woodside
Churnet View Road
Oakamoor
ST10 3AE

To Stuart, Iris and Albert.
All my love, Mumatron.

About the Author

In her career as a TV Producer working in magic & comedy Kirsty Smith introduced Russell Brand to an erotic lady wrestler, locked two presenters in a cage with 60 chickens for a week, and was made to magically appear dressed as a Morris Dancer from a giant pair of underpants. Now at home with two small children life is almost exactly the same but even funnier and with added rice cakes. She blogs at www.eehbahmum.com

Acknowledgements

Thanks to Grandma and Grandad aka Christine and Roger Smith for services to babysitting above and beyond the call of duty, staff on the Early Pregnancy Unit and the Birth Centre at Whittington Hospital, Lynn at the Active Birth Centre and all the wonderful people who have ever looked after my babies including Fiona Brennan, Claire Macina, Esscroft Nursery and Ben Rhydding Pre School. Thanks to my sister Rebecca for laughing down the phone at me when I had just given birth.

I have to say Thank You to all the wonderful followers of my blog who have read, liked and shared my nonsense online, Mumsnet and Netmums for supporting my work and James at Bennion Kearny for suggesting I might be able to write a book. I've met some annoyingly talented people whilst blogging especially 'People who are not shit' – thanks for all the jam, ladies, and of course a big shout out to all the bezzies for picking me up off the floor both literally and figuratively.

To Stuart for making all the plans and encouraging me to write and lastly to Iris and Albert for being the most fun I've ever had!

Chapter 1
This book is not...

I wrote this book for women like me. Career women who have decided it is time to start a family even though they really have no idea how babies and small children actually work. How hard can it be? I don't want you to lean in, have it all or stand on one leg and wave your arms about; this book is not going to tell you what to do. In fact, if you find it in the 'telling other people what to do' section of the bookshop please move it somewhere else - stick me in the cookery section instead, preferably near a book about pies. Mmmm pies.

This book is not a baby guide. There are plenty of books on that subject already, many of them written by people far more qualified than me. There are even a few written by people who are far less qualified than myself, probably best to move those to the fantasy section next to a book about dragons, ta.[1]

Most parenting books concentrate on the whole *having a baby thing* and I totally get that, it is quite a big part of becoming a mother. But I'm not here to reveal the best way to change a smelly nappy (quickly) or the secret to calming a teething baby (pickled onion Monster Munch) - I'm here to hold your hand and tell you it's all going to be okay. Which it definitely is. Probably.

---

[1] I know that, technically, asking you to rearrange the shelves of Waterstone's is sort of telling you what to do but I like to think of them as suggestions rather than orders. Whatevs.

The main worry I had about starting a family was not with the baby - I figured I could handle the whole looking-after-a-small-person business (I had woefully underestimated the amount of work involved with raising a child properly, by the way. More about that later). No, what concerned me more was how I would fit in having a baby with having a career. How was I going to keep up with work, maintain my friendships and care for a child of my own?

This book is about making the enormous gear change from being a successful professional to sitting at home changing nappies. As modern working women, we are used to organising other people, managing our time and finding solutions for tricky problems. We attack life and thrive on its many challenges because that's how we learn and improve and move on up that ladder. This book is for women who have survived demanding bosses, useless colleagues, and clients who expect the impossible. Hold on to all of that experience because having a baby is like working with all of those people rolled into one, and then some. If that sounds a little bit crazy, it's because it is. In a good way. Like most crazy things in life.

This book is not going to tell you how hard it is becoming a parent... I'm guessing you've already worked that bit out. Some parents like to tell you that it is the hardest thing you'll ever do, which is sort of true, but also a big fat lie. Nothing to do with having a baby is really hard work, because you're totally in love with it. Imagine working for a boss you were so smitten with they could literally vomit into your face and you'd still think they were amazing. I mean, I have had some pretty great bosses but I definitely think I would have drawn the line at them sitting on my knee and pooing on my J Brands.

As you can see, this book is also not going to give you a sugar-coated version of motherhood. I don't want to tell you that becoming a mother is the most natural thing a woman can do. I was in my late 30's when I had my first child. Meetings at Soho House were the most natural thing I could do... sitting in a circle at the library singing Incy Wincy Spider was as far from my natural habitat as I'd ever been.

The reality is that parenting is a crazy-assed mix of hard work and infinite love. Parenting is full of moments that push your emotional buttons and a lot of the time it's hard to know whether to laugh or cry. Most of the time, I choose to opt for laughing, and yes sometimes I am sort of laughing *at* my children but most of the time I'm laughing at me.

The me who spent all those years working hard, being organised, trying to ensure nothing went wrong in life, the same me who recently found herself sat on the floor of the cereal aisle at the supermarket trying to coax a three-year-old to let go of a giant box of cornflakes with Darth Vader on them for twenty minutes ("I find your lack of cornflakes disturbing"). Having a baby is the best fun you can have but it doesn't always look like much fun from the outside looking in.

The best illustration of real life parenting is this: I was sitting in the park one summer's day, watching my two-year-old daughter and baby son playing together in the sand pit and my eyes misted over at how lucky I was to have such beautiful children. Then I spotted something hanging out of my son's mouth and realised he was sucking a stranger's used sticking plaster. Before I could pull it out of his dribbling gob, my daughter face-planted into the ground and started screaming. A wailing toddler, a baby chewing scabs, and me wiping away tears of happiness whilst dry-retching into the sand pit. *That* is the truth about parenting. Plus you get to spend sunny days in the park. What's not to like?

This book is not going to tell you that motherhood changes you. It doesn't. Motherhood is life-changing but you, as a person, don't change. Even with a new-born baby, I was still the same potty-mouthed idiot I was before, but now with added rock hard tits that could explode at any minute and a super cute baby to distract people with. (I'm working on a film script about a group of lactating mums who use both these techniques to pull off elaborate heists.)

All the things you want to achieve in life do not miraculously disappear because you're a mum, your priorities simply shift a little; a tiny repositioning. You still have ambitions and interests, you can still drink and swear too much. If anything, the swearing increases with motherhood, until one day your daughter asks for 'fucking hummus' on her toast. Then it's time to stop.

If someone had told me, when I was working, that I would be on maternity leave for four years I would have stabbed them in the eye with a pencil. In my mind, becoming a proper mum was something that happened to other people; mums wore sensible clothes, mums did baking and cooking and crafts, mums were sublimely happy at home looking after babies. I knew I really wanted a baby, but the rest of that stuff? It didn't really grab me if I'm honest.

It still doesn't... four years on.

My children are the most important people in my life and I'm happy being a mum but there are still other things I want to do with my life. That hasn't changed.

This book is not going to ignore the real questions you have about becoming a mum. None of the baby books I looked at answered the questions I wanted answering. Mainly because they were all questions about me. Does that make me selfish? Probably, but at least I'm honest. Of course, I was worried about all the baby stuff but I was more concerned about what would happen to me. Am I going to enjoy this? Is it okay to be bored? Will all the other mums I meet be boring? Will I be boring? I'm not all that into babies... can I still have one? What if I'm shit at it? The simple answers to all these questions are: Yes, Yes, No, No, Yes and See Below for further details.

As someone who had flourished in the workplace my biggest fear was – what if I stop doing something I know I am good at to do something else and I am rubbish at it? There is no simple answer to this one; the truth of the matter is that you will be good at it *but not all the time.* You will lurch wildly from being awesome to being really bad on an almost hourly basis. Sometimes, when you are in the middle of making a celebratory cup of tea for being an amazing mum, your baby will fall over and bang his head and you will never get to drink your 'I'm an amazing mum!' beverage. You will have to swig a lukewarm cup of 'I am a terrible mother!' tea instead.

To be really happy as a mother you have to move expectations. Being a mum is not about being good at it; it isn't something you can 'win'. Having a baby that sleeps through the night, or feeds perfectly, or walks and talks first doesn't mean you are a better parent. Parenting is about getting on with whatever challenges present themselves that day.

So, this book is not going to tell you how you can have it all. Having it all looks like way too much hard work, the trick is to work out which bits are important to you and concentrate your efforts on those. I can definitely show you how to enjoy your time at home with a baby and, if you pay close attention, I'll teach you how to at least make it look like you have it all when you bump into that annoying woman from pregnancy yoga.

Chapter 2
Stupid things people say to women

If you make it past puberty without having yet reproduced, your family, colleagues (and people you stand next to at parties) will start to ask the inevitable 'When are you going to have children?' question. If you hit your thirties without starting a family, it is *literally* the only thing people want to know. Why is this? I have no idea. Maybe I am alone in thinking that what is going on in a woman's womb is nobody else's business unless it is causing a disturbance to neighbours at night. Clearly I am in the minority. Try to remember that every time a woman is asked *that* question a fairy gets punched in the ovaries with a brick, hard. So stop it, now! And while you're at it, tell your mum to stop it too. She's making Tinkerbell cry.

I developed a system based on those Argentinian restaurants where diners display a coloured disc to let the waiting staff know that they are open to receiving meat (green) or so full of meat they might be about to throw up (red). My reproductive flag system required women to wander around waving flags – red to let people know that their vagina is functioning recreationally only and green to alert passers-by that their womb is available for baby-making purposes. It was not a great success, in fact the whole system was abandoned as unworkable quite early on in the development process mainly because most women find constantly waving a flag to be quite tiring. Not to be dissuaded I am now working on a smaller-scale system reserved for younger members of the royal family who are great at flag waving *and* under constant baby-making scrutiny. Still awaiting the reply from Buckingham Palace.

One way to avoid *that* question is to burst into tears every time anyone asks you about your baby plans and spend the next three hours talking about your lady bits in glorious gynaecological detail. This is a surprisingly effective way to stop any future enquiries. However, the only foolproof way to stop people sticking their beaks into your baby business is to go ahead and get pregnant. I'm serious, whilst you are pregnant, at least no one is *asking* you if you are planning on getting pregnant. It's probably the best thing about being pregnant. Admittedly it's not ideal motivation for having a baby but it's also not the worst reason I've heard for starting a family.

Child: Mummy why did you have a baby?

Mum: Oh God, I don't know. Everyone just kept going on and on about it so I thought I should give it a go.

Child: A bit like Loom bands?

Mum: Yes darling, exactly like Loom bands but, with even more swearing and plastic shit all over the house.

But I have bad news for you – because once you've popped one sproglet out of your baby hole the question returns with great vengeance and furious anger, this time as 'Are you having any more?' I was asked if I'd be having another baby by one of the midwives while the placenta from my first baby was still pumping beside me.

Before I had children, I had a clearly defined list of things I thought were good parenting practice and things I thought were bad. The two were clearly delineated and obviously I would be doing all the good things – breastfeeding, baby-led weaning, learning through play – and none of the bad things - feeding them Haribo for breakfast, using the television as a babysitter, locking myself in the toilet and crying because I was bored off my tits. Before I had children, I was an idiot.

Now I have children I am still an idiot but I have less free time to reflect on this, which works out well for everyone.

There were certain things I assumed would happen when I started a family. No one actually sat me down and *said* these things would happen but I had seen them played out so often I just assumed they had some basis in fact. Idyllic scenes of family life are used to sell us mortgages, yoghurts and air fresheners. We see scenes of family perfection on television and in films starring Jennifer Aniston, Julia Roberts and Cameron Diaz and they're all total bollocks. Seriously, *The Lord of the Rings* is a more realistic portrayal of parenthood; in fact swap the One Ring for a ride-on-Police-Car and you've got the plotline for every stay and play session I've ever been to.

Here are some scenes you might recognise and some you won't. Yet.

Preparing for baby: sunlight streams through an open window onto a cot with a mobile hanging over it; mum-to-be (heavily pregnant wearing dungarees) paints the walls a shade of pastel; future dad playfully dabs paint on her nose, they hug and look around the room misty-eyed, imagining all the wonderful things that will happen there.

Reality Check: Mum-to-be is fat; sweaty, wearing leggings because Alexa Chung and the skinny girls now own all the dungarees. She sits on the floor of a spare bedroom piled with boxes and boxes of shit that need sorting/throwing out. Future dad is gripping onto a surfboard he bought whilst travelling, a surfboard that has fallen on and injured every single person who has ever stayed in the spare room, a surfboard which he thinks will make a 'nice feature' one day. It will not. (Unless he is planning on turning the spare room into a fantasy cocktail bar with a tropical beach theme rather than an actual nursery for an actual baby.) Both of you look around at all the rest of the crap in boxes you still have to argue about, bleary eyed, whilst imagining each other dead.

Saturday Morning: Mum wakes in bed, hair artfully dishevelled, sunlight streams through a window; she sees perfect dad bringing in a tray with coffee and the paper. Cute toddler carries a handpicked bloom from the garden 'For you Mummy!' They all sit up together with baby in beautiful crisp, white sheets and plan a fun-filled weekend together whilst nibbling bagels.

Reality Check: Christ where to start with this one? Mum opens her eyes and sees toddlers face staring directly into her own demanding she puts on *Peppa Pig*. It is still pitch black because it's 4am. Perfect Dad is missing, I mean actually missing. His side of the bed is empty but also mysteriously moist and smelling of sick. Mummy stumbles downstairs to find Daddy already half-asleep on the floor while the baby is sat in front of the telly. Everyone squashes under a duvet on the sofa and watches episodes of *Peppa Pig* eating cereal straight from the box. Repeat every weekend.

First Christmas: Basking in the festive glow of a roaring open fire, Daddy lifts up his precious baby girl to place the angel she made at Craftytime on top of the tree. Mummy and Daddy share a romantic kiss over a glass of Prosecco and start making plans for baby number two.

Reality Check: Are you mental? An open fire and a baby in the same room? Plus Daddy got overexcited at his first family Christmas and brought home a tree two feet taller than the lounge, someone (Mummy) has thrown away all the boxes of tree decorations in the great nursery purge and the angel that Daddy is so proud of was mostly made by a 60-year-old church volunteer. The entire festive season is spent trying to stop baby from climbing the tree and looking at photos from your old works' Christmas do on Facebook.

* * * * *

Basically nothing I thought about having a baby came true, there are many moments of perfection but there are also moments when you look at your partner and want to kill him although I think this probably happens even if you don't have children. So, really, what have you got to lose?

Having children turned out to be the best thing I've ever done, what I hadn't expected was the amount of fun involved, not boring fun like looking at a baby gurgling in a cot but actual proper fun like watching an 18-month-old walking repeatedly into a wall with a plastic bucket jammed on his head.

Before I had a baby I thought you had to be in the right place to have one, I thought I needed to live in a bigger home, find a more flexible job and at least be in a long term relationship. I compared my life to the lives of parents I knew and came to the conclusion that whatever it was you needed to start a family I didn't have it. So, I did what any sane person would do in this situation and waited for a magical fairy godmother to come along and sprinkle her sparkly, fairy dust over my life – transforming it into the perfect set up for having a baby. But the magic fairy was busy charging extortionate fees for children's birthday parties in the daytime and spending her cash buying up rotten teeth at night. Fairies are total idiots when it comes to money.

Meanwhile my career progressed, the hard work got harder, my home life grew more chaotic, and my wardrobe got more expensive. It made the idea of me becoming a parent seem even more ridiculous than it did when I was younger.

It's easy to look at parents of new-born children and see how completely different their lives are to yours. This is because the lives of new parents are extraordinary. A never-ending round of cooing over a tiny person with a face like an angry walnut who stops both Mummy and Daddy from doing anything fun anymore.

Most parents of new-born babies have a terrified, exhausted look as though they have spent the night in a haunted house. New parents make having a baby look like *really* hard work, no one in their right minds looks at parents with a new-born baby and thinks 'Whoo! Yeah! Get me a small demanding person to drag around with me – everywhere – who keeps me up all night! That looks awesome!' Watching your favourite happy couple bicker and snipe over the correct way to fasten the poppers on a baby grow is just depressing and, let's face it, when your *work* is hard work you don't really need to make being at home hard work too.

What you don't get to see from the outside is the immense feeling of love that a parent has for their children. As soon as you have your own baby, something 'kicks in' that transforms a crying wrinkly little person – that looks a bit like Alan Sugar having a poo – into the most amazing thing you've ever seen. You don't fall in love with your own children like you do with other people, they just rock up one day and it's a done deal.

Basically becoming a parent is a massive mind fuck which you cannot really prepare for – a bit like one of those crazy parties where *everything* happens; everyone who went feels like death, someone books a foreign holiday with a complete stranger, and none of you can really explain what happened to people who weren't there, but everyone knows it was worth it.

Before I had children, I wasn't really a baby person. Today, I don't really know what a baby person is anymore but I definitely thought that there were women out there that really liked babies and I knew I was not one of them.

Before I had children I wasn't really all that into babies but now I've had two I like them more. But only my own and, even then, mainly when they're sleeping.

I should probably point out that I've never hated babies. I was just... unaffected by them. If there was a baby being passed around a room, sure, I'd have a hold of it but only to make the point that I wasn't scared of it (which by the way, I totally was). I assumed you had to be 'into babies' to enjoy being a mum but the surprising truth about becoming a mother is that you can actually be a bit 'meh' about children and still go on to enjoy being a parent.

Holding your cousin's baby at a wedding and secretly wanting to swap it for a full glass of champagne after 20 seconds does not mean you're not good with babies. It just means there is champagne. Champagne trumps babies every time. Why do you think Mum is passing the baby around in the first place?

In fact, people who find babies a bit boring and annoying are more prepared for parenthood than people who think babies are amazing ickle cute snuggly things. People who are 'into babies' must have a terrible time when they actually get one of their own. Anyone who labours under the misapprehension that babies are cute is in for an almighty shock when they discover what babies do for the rest of the day. 'Oh, I'm sorry, did she ruin your sofa?'

When couples are considering starting a family they'll often try their parenting skills out on other people's babies to see if they should have a go. This is a mistake. Other people's children are almost always awful. I have two wonderful children that I love dearly and I still don't like other people's babies, although now at least I can spend time in the same room as them without getting the fear.

There are good reasons why other people's babies are not the ideal testing ground for the shall-we-have-a-family experiment. Babies make noise and smells and that's about it; apart from pulling awesome poo faces, their CV is pretty much a blank page. This is fine because children are only babies for about 18 months of their lives, then they mutate into tiny angry little people, before becoming more like proper people (but still useless). So, there's really nothing to test yourself with. You can offer to feed it if there's a bottle around (don't offer to breastfeed someone else's baby) and you can offer to change a nappy but neither of these acts will help you decide if you really want a baby. People who know how to change nappies or bath babies don't have a head start on those that can't. The big secret about starting a family is that even if you are not really the baby type, you can still totally rock it as a parent. In fact, it is perfectly okay to not be completely certain about starting a family before you go for it. Who is ever completely certain about any big decision in life? Buying houses, having babies, changing jobs – only stupid people or the insanely rich are not affected by these things.

My partner and I were both very much in the undecided camp for the entire time I was pregnant and then, once labour started, I moved firmly into the 'this is a bad, bad idea camp' before pushing and panting my way into probably the best decision I have ever made camp (although I was off my face on Etonox and exhaustion by this point). Since having my children I have repeatedly moved between all three of these camps on a weekly basis.

If other babies and parents are bad for testing the water then toddlers are even worse. In fact, if you are seriously considering starting a family I would recommend ignoring the whole part where they mutate from babies into little boys and girls. Seriously, just try to block out a whole two-year period in child development. I mean obviously it's going to happen but thinking about it is not going to make it any less painful... so why bother?

Toddlers are off the chart crazy. Imagine your most high-maintenance friend – you know the one, the friend who always has a starring role in all your best stories. Now imagine she's just found out she's been cheated on and passed over for promotion on the same day. Hide the posh wine glasses and prepare yourself for several months of carnage. Crazy nights mixed with afternoons crying on the sofa watching *Gossip Girl* and eating *all* the biscuits. When you both come out of the other side you'll have some unbelievable tales to tell, your sofa will be covered in red wine stains and you'll never be able to face the neighbours again. Swap *Gossip Girl* for *Postman Pat* and the red wine stains for every other stain you can imagine and that is *exactly* what dealing with toddlers is like.

Toddlers are completely unpredictable which is part of their charm but also the reason why my face is way more wrinkly now I have kids. Half of it I put down to stress but the other half is laughing, so I can't really complain. My son had very specific plate requirements as a toddler – sometimes he could only eat off a green plate but at any given point this could change and he might require a red plate. Sometimes this change would happen *in the middle of eating his lunch* which was sort of fine when he was eating sandwiches but quite messy if we were having pasta. If you were to see him in action, you would think he was being quite rude when, in fact, he was just being two, and sometimes two year olds are awful.

Basically, other people's toddlers will put you off parenting forever. Try to block that bit out completely and if you do ever meet up with friends, and their toddlers, know that it's perfectly okay to come home and cry.

If you can handle a heartbroken 30-year-old who's downed half a bottle of tequila and just ruined her favourite Marc Jacobs dress then you can cope with a small child. Essentially it's the same skill set, clean up the mess, wipe away the tears, and let them know that you love them even though you don't always approve of how they're handling situations. At least when a toddler starts crying on the floor in Starbucks you will attract more sympathetic looks.

There are things you can do to prepare for parenthood that are more practical than putting yourself in close contact with actual children. The first thing you should sort out is learning to have in-depth personal conversations with total strangers. No, really.

People love dishing out advice to parents and parents-to-be. In fact, the minute your pregnancy begins to show, people in the supermarket queue will start giving you unwanted advice about breastfeeding, or weaning, or a million-and-one other things you have literally *no idea* about. Don't worry about reading all the books... just stand around Sainsbury's with a baby bump and wait for complete strangers with a trolley full of Muller Corners to tell you what to do.

It's quite normal for people to stop you and tell you about all kinds of helpful things when you have a baby. Mostly people are trying to be helpful. Unfortunately, strangers telling the owner of a crying baby that their child needs swaddling/feeding/more sleep is of no help to a frazzled new mum and just adds to the feeling of panic and helplessness (as though everyone else knows what to do but you).

Even better are the inevitable horror tales about childbirth, just in case you weren't worried enough about the whole thing. 'My friend spent three weeks in labour, in the end they had to chisel the baby out with a rusty butter knife in the hospital car park because there were no beds. There was no time for an epidural so the midwife just punched her unconscious with her bare fists.'

I may have exaggerated slightly but wait and see. The best bit is once you're the size of a house you are both easy to spot and unable to waddle away with any speed. At any other time, had someone started prodding me and asking personal questions about the sex of something inside me I would have told them to get lost but it seemed unbecoming of a mother-to-be to be seen shouting angrily at people in the street.

Hah! Now that I *am* a mother I'd say that at least 20 percent of my waking hours are spent shouting angrily at people in the street. The only difference is that I only ever shout at people who have seen the inside of my vagina. Everyone else I just ignore.

Chapter 3
How having a baby is exactly like being at work. And how it isn't

Once upon a time, there was a beautiful Princess who moved to the big city where she met a handsome Prince. This Prince was better than all those other Princes as he had a good job with great career prospects, and he took the beautiful Princess out for dinner to nice restaurants. She dreamed of them living together in a castle one day.

But the path of true love did not run smooth. Maybe the Princess had been cursed by a wicked witch, perhaps she'd been fed magic beans by an evil giant or possibly she'd just been born unlucky. For yes, the Princess was cursed. And once she kissed (ahem) the handsome Prince he was transformed into a terrible bell end, which is way worse than a frog. At least if that had happened she'd have made the pages of *Take A Break*. As well as being a bell end he also had commitment issues and actually – when you *really* looked properly at him – he wasn't even all that handsome so the beautiful Princess dumped him and found herself another Prince. Alas, he too turned out to be a bit of a dick, and the next one, and the next. Honestly what is wrong with the world today?

Just when the beautiful Princess was about to give up on her happily-ever-after she realised that there was someone else who loved her. Someone who had been there for her all along, someone she loved more than all the Princes in the land. That someone else was her career. Her career had never been spotted getting over-friendly with a blonde in Nando's, or ignored her phone calls for three whole weeks. In fact, her job had helped her to buy nice shoes and provided her with wine, it had even taken her away on trips to foreign lands and once to the Jury's Inn in Cardiff for a whole two weeks. More importantly, her job meant that she could buy her own teeny tiny London flat that cost almost the same as a castle. So, Fuck You handsome Princes.

And that should have been the end of it, a far better finale to the modern fairy tale than 'they all lived happily ever after', but it wasn't the end.

Like every successful story told these days, there's a badly-plotted sequel where loads of crazy unexpected shit happens totally ruining the original tale for everyone who bought into it. The beautiful Princess met another handsome Prince (will she never learn!) whilst drunk in a field and she started cheating on her career with him. In no time at all, the beautiful Princess got pregnant and she found herself having to turn her back on the thing she once loved. What the hell was she supposed to do now?

This modern fairy tale is being played out all across the land. Women today are encouraged to work hard and have everything that men have. There's no more waiting for Mr Right to come along; we're down with the fact that it's up to us to sort ourselves out. In fact, we actually quite like doing it thank you very much. But there's one big difference between men and women – however hard they try, men can't have babies. Men also have appalling taste in duvet covers. Have you ever known a man who could choose a decent duvet cover? I think not. But while you can accidentally give away a Playboy bedding set to the charity shop there's no getting around the having a baby stuff, so it's up to us women to get on with it as best we can.

Before I had children, I worked in television producing magic and comedy shows. Like most people with a 'good job' I was used to working hard and putting in long hours. I missed family funerals, friends' weddings and my own birthdays because I had to work (NB: you still get a year older even if you don't have a party). I didn't choose to work hard because it was expected of me, or because I had to prove a point, I worked hard because my work was interesting, exciting and challenging and I didn't mind one bit – I loved it.

And then I had a baby and work just didn't work for me anymore. So I decided not to go back and made the gigantic leap from career girl to stay at home mum. I left full time employment four years ago and have spent the majority of my time since then, at home, looking after two small children; I chose to put my career on hold to stay at home and teach my children to walk and talk and not lick station platforms to see what trains taste like. I chose not to return to full time work mainly because we are lucky and could afford for me to do this but at least once a day I miss work, usually when I'm in the toilet explaining why Mummies have hairy bottoms to my 'colleagues'. *That* never happened in my last job.

Don't get me wrong, when I was in work I spent most of my time moaning about it – the long hours, the annoying workmates and the difficult bosses. But as well as a reason to get up every morning (and go drinking every week night) – working gives you an identity. When I was working, I used my job to define myself, I was proud of what I did and I liked being identified as that short Northern girl who produces telly. Okay, if I'm really honest I could have lived without the short bit but I've finally accepted that a growth spurt is no longer on the cards.

Now that I am at home with small children, if someone uses my 'work' to define me – my face turns a funny shade of purple. When I signed up for a new Doctors surgery after having my daughter, the doctor's receptionist (nothing good ever follows those two words) enquired if she should put me down as a 'house wife' or a 'home maker'? I nearly passed out in horror. I simply did not, correction DO NOT identify with either of these descriptions. For starters, I'm not married (and we lived in a flat) so that's the first one out of the running ('flat girlfriend' was not an option, I checked). And don't get me started on home maker, just put me down as freelance.

Six months earlier, I had been in charge of budgets and teams meeting deadlines... I had spreadsheets! Now I realised that if something horrible happened and I ended up on the news, I would be described by my relationship to other people. Somewhere along the line, my previous identity had been wiped out by the simple act of giving birth. Not only had this baby given me a sore fanny and a fat arse, it had also erased my entire life's achievements. Well done baldy.

* * * * *

Anyone with a successful career will look to their professional skills to see which ones are transferable when they start a family. It makes absolute sense to take things you have learned through work and apply them to having a baby. It's only natural to approach having a baby as the next big project, researching and planning it out. The problem is that babies are not like work, I mean they are totally like work but in a completely different way. But there are skills that will transfer from a successful career to parenting. And some that won't.

Leadership. The problem with leadership skills is that you're not the leader any more, you are the most senior member of staff on the team and the person with ultimate responsibility, but you are very much at the beck and call of a young new boss with crazy ideas and terrible personal hygiene. Remember how frustrating it was when crap Karen got promoted above you and she was useless and you ended up having to do everything and then she had the audacity to spend her lunch hour crying on your shoulder because she couldn't cope? It's a bit like that but without the lunch hour.

If you really miss having people to delegate to, why not put yourself in charge of crapping, and throwing up, and tell everyone you've 'delegated' these roles to the baby. Top leadership skills in action.

Problem Solving. Modern career girls are used to dealing with problems, we find creative and innovative ways around difficulties all the time, we are used to making things that don't work, work. When life gives us lemons we don't make lemonade, we invest a lot of time and a great deal of effort into swopping those shitty, bitter lemons for lovely sweet grapes to make wine instead. Because we don't want lemonade we want wine, most of my friends are pretty much unstoppable when there is wine on offer.

This torturous drinks analogy is supposed to illustrate the fact that before I started a family I assumed that through hard work and determination I could solve any problem and achieve anything I wanted. Budgets that are too small, timescales that are too short, lazy colleagues and crazy bosses – all of these work 'problems' could be overcome by hard work and a logical and analytical approach.

Handling the problems thrown up by a teeny person with no access to email looked easy from the outside. But the simple process of attacking a problem until it is solved is a recipe for total disaster when babies and small children are involved.

This is advice I have learnt the hard way. When my daughter was first born I kept a logbook of all her feeds so, if there were any problems, I would be able to show it to the doctor who would immediately diagnose the problem and award me full marks for being an ace parent. Except there was absolutely nothing wrong with my daughter and the notes just started to stress me out as I realised there was no pattern whatsoever to my baby's feeds. Eventually I showed the midwife my research and she diagnosed panicky new mum syndrome and told me to chuck the book in the bin and read a magazine instead.

Babies don't have issues that need resolving. They just *are*, they just *do*, they stay awake at night just because, they cry just because, they feed, they poo, they sleep erratically because they can and just when you think you've got a handle on things they completely change their whole routine. Just because. Babies are unpredictable little fuckers.

Trying to develop a strategy to manage them, or planning a course of action, might make you feel better but you'd be just as effective sitting down having a nice cup of tea, reading *Grazia*, and accepting that although your new boss knows cock all about anything – they are in charge and you might as well lump it. And they do have a lovely, squishy bottom.

Work Ethic. This one absolutely transfers. Parents of small children are always keen to point out that having a baby is hard work, as though people without children have no concept of hard work. The truth of the matter is that having a baby is no more hard work than having a demanding job – both of them mess up your social life and leave your home looking a mess. In fact, if anything, it's more motivating looking after a child – imagine how much more exciting work would be if you were totally in love with your boss/colleague but in a way that wouldn't end up at a tribunal.

Teamwork. Babies make terrible work colleagues as they have appalling interpersonal skills. Your baby is basically the equivalent of the big boss's son that time he came on work placement – absolutely useless but no one dares say anything about it for fear it will reflect badly on them. At home, the baby is the only other member of your team and not only are they not pulling their weight they are actively making things worse for you. Being at home with a baby would be way easier without the baby. I would have aced parenting if it weren't for the kids.

Negotiation and Persuasion. There are some schools of thought that say you should never negotiate with a small child but these people are missing out on a whole world of fun. There is nothing more fun than arguing with a toddler about the *exact* number of peas they have to eat before they are allowed a biscuit.

In my former career as a TV Producer I spent a lot of time dealing with agents. Negotiating with a three-year-old is very much the same as dealing with an agent but a small child is unlikely to call you a c*nt and slam the phone down. Almost all negotiations you have will be about biscuits, chocolate or otherwise, and every single negotiation will end with a small child consuming more biscuits than you had at first intended. If you decide the limit is two biscuits they will invariably end up eating at least five, with a break after the third biscuit for tears and a foot stomping.

Ability to Work under Pressure. This is where your change in circumstances is felt most sharply. Before I had a baby, I was pretty confident and capable in most stressful situations. Fast forward just a few weeks when, as a new mum, I tried to sign for an Amazon delivery whilst balancing a baby in one arm and shovelling a nipple back into a maternity bra. Frankly, it brought me to the verge of tears. The trick is to accept that the bar has been lowered – where once you might feel a sense of inner pride for dealing with a particularly difficult client now you award yourself a whole packet of Jaffa Cakes when you sign for a *Gossip Girl* DVD.

Organisation. Perfect preparation might prevent pisspoor performance, but try telling a baby that. At work, you might have been the one who was never late for a meeting and hit every deadline but once you have a baby you are given a free pass to rock up late everywhere you go. If the thought of being late and surrounded by chaos fills you with horror then don't worry, it is possible to be completely organised and look after a baby but you will need to factor in breaks during the day so you can cry with exhaustion and/or frustration in the toilet. Or you could just accept that now you're a mum you will be forever rocking up 10 minutes late wearing dirty jeans. Take your pick.

I went from micromanaging every last detail of a project to literally forgetting to cover up my boobs in public.

Becoming a mum is the perfect time to take a step back and look at the bigger picture. Is my baby still alive? Did I put clothes on when I left the house? Will that stain come out with a baby wipe? If you can answer yes (or probably) to these questions then you're winning.

So many first time mums have amazing plans and projects for their maternity leave. I spent the last few weeks of my pregnancy researching Mandarin Chinese lessons, which I was going to fit in around training for my first marathon and writing a novel. I have not even started any of these things although I did recently finish watching every single episode of *Gossip Girl* so it's not been a complete waste of time.

Becoming a parent for the first time is an exhausting, exciting and rewarding ride, just like any great career – and the best thing is you don't even have to have an interview! But before you get your happy-ever-after there's the tiny matter of giving birth...

Chapter 4
Enjoy the baby bubble, it won't last forever

But first a bit about childbirth…

When you find out you are pregnant, you will go round all your friends who have already had babies and ask them to retell their birth story and spare none of the squeamish bits. They will have already told you this story in full glorious detail several times before but you will never have really listened to what they're saying the way you will when you are about to have a baby yourself. Your fabulous friends will spend a long time reliving their experience of childbirth with ALL the gory details and after each tale you will be left with the same unanswered question. 'But what is it actually *like?*'

The brutal truth is that no one knows what childbirth will be like for you. People can share their stories and experiences but there is no way of knowing how it will play out for you, however much you prepare. Childbirth can be a dark cloud looming all through your pregnancy; you can read books and blogs and watch television shows with huffing and puffing and groaning and panting and none of it will really explain what the hell is going to happen to you. The main thing to accept about childbirth is that you can have a preference for the type of birth you want but it's not something you can demand. You can laminate a million copies of your birth plan, ask all the questions and brief everyone involved about what you want to happen, but on the day be prepared to just go with the flow.

Let's be frank about this. If we could choose what we wanted we'd have babies delivered in a lovely black box wrapped in tissue and ribbon like a Net A Porter parcel. Unfortunately, that is not an option available to us.

Yet.

So just stick to getting that baby out the best way you can and then order yourself a present as a prize.

The ideal person to answer all your questions is a friend who has been through it, but be careful! It is important to choose your baby mentor wisely – you need someone you can trust to be honest but who isn't going to get carried away and leave you terrified. That's not to say you should avoid friends with a flair for the dramatic, you are going to be at home with a baby so having a friend who is a complete drama queen will make for brilliant coffee dates. Just don't rely on them to fill you in on the nitty gritty of childbirth.

The best people to speak to are new mums, someone just a few months further down the line than you, someone who still winces when they sit down. New mums are perfectly positioned to pass on all the stuff they've learned while it is fresh in their minds. A mum who has just had a baby will understand more than a mum with older children because (and here's a big secret) – parents forget shit. I am amazed at how quickly I forgot stuff. There was just 20 months between my two children and I couldn't remember a bloody thing second time round. Basically parents only remember events that were either really traumatic or totally hilarious which means that you only ever hear horror stories or cute tales – all of which starts to make parenting feel a bit like the auditions for *Britain's Got Talent*.

I cannot remember when either of my children started to sleep through the night or began talking but I clearly remember when my son started walking because he fell into the same garden shrub three times in one day, which was both traumatic (for him) and hilarious (for me).

Parenting amnesia is also why you should never trust anything Grandparents say; anything anyone tells you about a baby they had over twenty years ago should be taken with a pinch of salt – it might be true or it may have been a plotline on *Eastenders*, we'll never know. My Grandma used to tell stories about clocking off at the chicken factory to go sit in the pub with Sting. Actual Sting. My Grandma was brilliantly crackers. Unfortunately, she was not around by the time I had children so I missed out on her parenting wisdom which no doubt would have been equally enlightening/useless.

If I could turn back time like Cher or Doctor Who[2] the main thing I would do differently in childbirth would have been to book acting lessons for my fella. Not that I wanted the soliloquy from Hamlet as I rolled around the floor on all fours but it would have been more entertaining than staring into his horrified face. If your partner really wants to get involved, have him practice his 'not looking terrified' face in the mirror; oh and if anyone else has an opinion on how you should be giving birth, remember it's perfectly acceptable to tell them politely to cock off. I said so.

I wanted a natural childbirth. I got a natural childbirth and a handful of stitches. At one point there were three whole midwives staring at my ruined vagina discussing which bits went where, meanwhile I was beaming with pride feeding

---

[2] actually If I could turn back time this is not a time I would choose to revisit '*Skip the party with the Mitfords or the chance to hang out with the Bronte sisters I want to go back to that time when I shit myself in a bath whilst mooing like a cow.*' **

** Yeah that does happen. Sorry.

my rather fantastic new daughter with my actual boob (yes it is a bit weird at first). The important piece of take out information from this paragraph is not the stitching but the fact that I was totally enraptured whilst this was going on. And I hadn't even taken all the drugs!

Giving birth is an extreme experience. My partner told me it was the most amazing thing he'd ever seen although, admittedly, this was before series 7 of *Breaking Bad* came out on DVD. I don't think he was referring to the particularly impressive way I gave birth just the actual act of bringing a baby into the world.

I can't explain what giving birth is going to be like for you – no one can, but I can tell you that the rewards for all your efforts are immense even if they do make a lot of noise and bad smells. If your birth goes to plan then be happy about that. If your birth goes horribly off plan then congratulate yourself even more for coping and understand that things going terribly off plan is pretty much what's in store for the next few years. However you get that baby out, take time to stop and think about what you've done and congratulate yourself on how embarrassingly awesome you are. Champagne all round! (extra ice for your poor fanny).

* * * * *

A bit about breastfeeding or not, whatevs. Your choice.

Before I start I should make it clear that I couldn't give a flying monkey how you choose to feed your baby – if you're going with bottles feel free to skip the next few pages. Basically the rest of this chapter is just me saying 'tits' a lot and moaning about my nipples… so you're not missing out on much. All I ask is that you remember that however you choose to do it, just know that the mums doing it differently to you are having an equally tough time of it. Also, people sometimes don't even get to make a choice, so when you see a mum feeding a small baby with a bottle or a boobie give them a supportive smile (but don't wink 'cos apparently some people find that a bit weird).

I found that there were some people so desperate for you to give breastfeeding a go that they 'forgot' to tell you it's actually really hard work and frankly a little bit weird. I don't mean that I find breastfeeding in any way unnatural, I just mean it's an out-of-the-ordinary thing to do for any woman who has spent most of her life *not* sticking her nipples in someone else's mouth.

I breastfed both my babies for over a year and the one thing I can honestly tell you is that it does get easier with time. By the time my second baby was a month old I had mastered the art of feeding him whilst stood up in the pouring rain on the bank of the Thames drinking Pimms and waving at The Queen (she didn't wave back).

If this was my finest breastfeeding hour, it's hard to choose my lowest breastfeeding moment. Perhaps it was sending my partner out to buy organic cabbage to stick in my bra because I was convinced the pesticides in a non-organic cabbage would make my baby ill? The time I chatted to a young man clearing tables in a cafe with my entire left boob hanging out? Ah no! How about that time I got the fear in a busy City cafe when I realised I was the only person not wearing a smart suit, and I'm sure someone tutted because my pram was in the way, and then I couldn't find my purse in the huge changing bag full of baby crap, and I swear someone sighed – so I locked myself in the bathroom and sat on the loo crying and feeding and sweating and crying some more. Hmm, it's hard to choose.

Now I'm a mum of toddlers I'm all sweary confidence and kick ass attitude. But in the early days? Remember a lot of what is happening is out of your control because of hormones. So if you're going to enjoy the ride, try to chill out as best you can. Your mantra should be: This too shall pass. Oh and the cabbage thing works.

One of the main things I didn't love about breastfeeding were the clothes I had to wear. Yes, I am that shallow. But it's the truth. I'd spent several months wearing giant pants and floaty tops and I wanted to wear clothes that made me feel good. Nursing outfits do not make anyone feel good. Any clothes suitable for breastfeeding are all subject to one rule; forget Does it fit? or Is this my colour? The golden rule is this: How quickly can I get my nipples out of these clothes and into another person's mouth?

Thinking about it, this might not be the first time you have ever asked yourself this question when shopping so let me add some clarification: How quickly can I get my nipples out of these clothes and into another person's mouth *in Costa Coffee*? If you have ever asked yourself this on a shopping trip then you are seriously going to ROCK breastfeeding.

Here is a (non-exhaustive) list of things that are impractical to wear when you are breastfeeding: dresses with long sleeves, dresses with short sleeves, shirts/ blouses with fiddly buttons, any tops in grey marl or silk.

Most dresses are a no-no because unless they have thin straps or wrap around, you have to pull them completely up over your body to access your funbags exposing all your lovely post-baby wobbly bits. No thanks. Shirts or blouses with buttons involve a great deal of fiddling about in order to get boob access and silk or grey marl will show off any embarrassing nipple leakage to maximum effect. Also, breastfeeding can make you really sweat adding dark armpit stains to the milky boob marks. Neither milky boob or sweaty armpit stains got a mention in Alexa Chung's style bible so let's take it from AC that they're out.

Breastfeeding is hard work, it can be painful, and you may have to wear sanitary towels in your bra (I know! Who even knew these things existed?) so it's vitally important to give yourself a big pat on the back when you do manage to breastfeed a child whether you do six days, six weeks or six months. Every day you manage it – *you're a winner*. A winner wearing a horrible tunic top that smells a bit like a warm yogurt.

Now let's get started with the really fun bit.

* * * * *

When you finally arrive home from hospital with a newborn baby, your entire world feels as though it's been turned upside down. Bits of you have. The car journey home from hospital is the most terrifying car journey you will ever take. At least on the way to the hospital you have contractions to distract you, on the way back you really get to focus properly on being terrified at the thought of looking after a baby.

Back at home, simple everyday things that you used to do without a second thought become almighty challenges; it's like starting all over again, learning how to do simple tasks with a baby in tow while a terrifying sense of responsibility weighs you down. Emotionally and physically exhausted for the first few weeks, everything seems like such a momentous effort.

What made things worse was that all around me were cards and flowers from friends and family who already had children – they all seemed to have managed perfectly well, going about their lives and producing children with the minimum of fuss. How the hell had we never noticed what a momentous thing they had done? I remembered stories friends had glibly told me about emergency c-sections, babies in special care, mums kept in hospital for days after the labour. All we had done was go into hospital, have a 'normal' birth and return home and I still felt completely overwhelmed with it all.

Welcome to the baby bubble! The baby bubble is a wonderful time bathing in the complete love you have for your new arrival and absolute fear of the outside world and all the bad things that are out there. Remember to take time out from being scared and exhausted to enjoy yourself with your new baby, and by enjoy yourself I do mean sitting, staring at your sleeping baby weeping into their tiny little face thinking what the hell have we done?

Don't worry... this doesn't last forever! Well actually it sort of does, but the sheer terror of it all soon passes. The underlying love that causes you to be so scared – that doesn't ever go away, even when you are screaming at a two-year-old to stop hitting his big sister in the face with a wooden train. Deep down you could still pull his pants down, bite into his squishy bum and tell him he's got the best bottom in the world. Almost. Oh did I mention that becoming a parent can send you slightly crackers?

There are lots of different theories on when and how you should deal with visitors in the early days, but let's face it this will probably be determined by the relationships you already have with friends and family. Just make sure you let people know that normal rules for guests are suspended – the house will be a mess and you may have to make your own cup of tea. Also, they should bring biscuits, posh ones. The best rule of thumb is to do what makes you feel happy, and whatever happens *do not tidy up*. You will be tidying up for many years to come so don't waste your first few days with your precious baby cleaning up for visitors. You have a gorgeous cute little person to show off so who cares if there are underpants drying on the radiators? Sit back and enjoy your time together and if anyone is stupid enough to ask if there's anything they can do, point them in the direction of the kitchen.

However you handle those early days, at some point you are going to be left at home on your own with your baby. I spent my first morning posing with my daughter in front of the bathroom mirror like she was an expensive new dress. I practised introducing myself to people as a mum – *What this thing in the pram? IT'S A BABY! I'M A MUM! I MADE A BABY! LOOK AT IT! SHE'S PERFECT!'* Thankfully, I was home alone so no one knows I did this because that would be totally embarrassing.

Fortunately, most mums are too busy to waste too much time making a tit of themselves. But busy doing what? Seriously, what the hell do new mums get up to all day? We've all read a million magazine articles following A Day In The Life Of... I'd read about CEOs, designers, human rights lawyers, environmental activists and award-winning physicists but I didn't have a bloody clue what a mum with a new baby did all day. No one does. Until they do it and even then you're still a bit unsure of where the day went.

Before children, a typical day might look like this: a session at the gym, followed by a morning in meetings and debriefs, grabbing lunch at your desk then catching up with a few friends for dinner after work. Somewhere amongst all this you dropped off your dry cleaning, picked up some shopping, booked a hotel for your friend's birthday weekend away and argued with your boyfriend by email *and* phone.

Go you! Now you're at home, alone with a baby - let's start by making a sandwich or having a shower.

I'd love to tell you that I'm exaggerating for comic effect but I once ate dry bread, a whole tomato and nibbled a block of cheese straight from the fridge because I hadn't mastered the art of preparing food with one hand whilst feeding a baby. If you really want to do something practical to prepare for starting a family try learning to get through the day with one hand tied behind your back and someone crying and puking into your face.

In those early weeks at home with a new baby, time slows down. Suddenly it's the end of the day and your partner is home and you appear to have achieved nothing. Over the next few weeks you will slowly build up your skill set, and work out how to have a shower, how to dress yourself, you might even manage to brush your hair and put on some mascara (stick to waterproof mascara while the hormones are still high). At some point, you will eventually make it out of the house. It will take you for ever.

Your partner will come home and you'll proudly announce that you managed to get yourself and the baby washed and dressed and out to the doctors on time without crying and he'll shrug his shoulders as though it's no big deal. Try not to punch him in the face when he does this. Because it is a big deal. Everything you do as a new parent is hard work. Even the most basic of tasks are being done whilst feeding, cleaning and nurturing a whole other person. Every day you make it through with or without crying you are winning. There's a lot of winning in this book; most of my parenting involves simply telling myself I'm doing fine.

Beware of daytime television; that shit will screw you up! Up until I had my babies, watching *This Morning* posed no particular challenge for me but in the postnatal fug of hormones a simple makeover report could have me in floods of tears. Do not even consider watching the news or charity telethons. When my son was born, I watched *Schindler's List* for the first time and my partner had to come home from work early because I was such a mess. Again… hormones! But one day you *will* be able to make it through a whole episode of *This Morning* without crying your way through half a loo roll watching Gino make a particularly nice lasagne.

Remember the new baby mantra: This too shall pass.

For the first few days with a baby, it feels like you are drowning in emotions moving violently from glowing happiness to dry retching through fear. On top of the physical and emotional shit storm, there's the stress of being a parent for the first time; aside from the stinging, the biggest sensation I felt after giving birth was sheer panic. All those questions I had before I started a family were still there, still unanswered.

What if I'm shit at this? What if I'm shit at this and everyone can tell? What if I'm so shit at this people start laughing and pointing at me in the street? What if I dropped it or broke it? What if I kept calling her 'it' for the rest of our lives? Surely good parents didn't refer to their precious newborns as 'it' for the first month? (Er, they do).

I don't know anyone who didn't have these thoughts in the first few days and the brilliant answer to all these questions is that the very fact you are asking them and worrying about this stuff means you are being a good parent. It's perfectly normal to be absolutely shit scared about the enormity of the tasks in front of you. If I could give one line of advice to new parents it would be to chill the fuck out, I appreciate that's not the most supportive thing to say, and I'm sorry, but it's the key to parenting.

Chilling the fuck out is easier to do if you can let go of your pre-baby self – the woman who did things and went places – not forever, but just while you're in the baby bubble. All the time I was struggling with a baby, my former self was there watching, my pre-baby self simply couldn't understand how I was struggling with all this simple stuff. That's because my pre-baby self was a bit of a judgemental twat. These days I am much kinder on myself because I know that actually having a baby is a big thing to do, and, yes, simple tasks do seem difficult for a time and that's fine. It's not forever.

I expected some natural magical mothering force to unleash itself, and I would instinctively know what to do. But that never happened. Instead of becoming a 'mum' I was exactly the same person but less confident and with crazy, milky breasts and a baby to look after. So I did what everybody does when they have an embarrassing medical complaint and are looking for meaning in the world, I turned to the

Internet and took advice from complete strangers with names like glittermum76 and spanglesmcbooby.

Basically, I Googled the crap out of having a baby.

Amazingly this turned out to be the right thing to do. Perhaps I did have that natural mothering instinct after all! Online I found people asking the same questions I was asking although without all the swear words. Turns out I didn't actually need most of my questions answering I just needed to know that I wasn't the only one asking them.

Remember that doing mum shit all day is hard work and very unrewarding so don't be afraid congratulate yourself for life's tiny victories. Chill the fuck out and enjoy the baby bubble, it doesn't last for long and once you're out the other side you'll be back to your ass-kicking former self.

But first you're going to need a posse...

Chapter 5
How to make friends that aren't really, really, boring

From the outside looking in, groups of new mums sitting around in cafes chatting about how many times they were up last night and the consistency of little Mabel's poo are – hmmm, how to put this – boring! If you're throwing your arms up in horror at this statement I'm sorry but I really think you might be reading the wrong book.

If you're worried that it will be dull hanging out with a load of baby bores then I've got bad news. You are going to be a baby bore yourself. Maybe just for a few weeks, maybe a few months, but it will happen. And guess what? The world won't end. Becoming a baby bore was pretty high up on my list of things I was never going to do. Today, I wonder why. The very fact that I thought mums were baby bores makes me a little embarrassed. So what if new mothers go on about their babies a bit too much? It's totally natural to be all encompassed by motherhood at first; that's kinda how it's meant to work.

'Oh I'm sorry do I keep blathering on about how I've created a brand new human fucking being using just my womb and a teaspoon of sperm? I do apologise, you must tell me more about how the guy you share a desk with keeps taking two hour lunch breaks because that is, in no way, dull as shit.'

Basically, when you have a baby, your priorities change. Whereas you once found the sleeping patterns of a six-week-old human interminably dull, now you find them more exciting than a *Game Of Thrones* marathon. It's those hormones again.

I say *be* 'a baby bore', embrace the time you spend together; in no time at all you'll look up and out and start to notice the rest of the world again. The rest of the world will have been carrying on in exactly the same way it always does and you won't have missed a thing and I promise you will never regret a single moment you spent with your baby or talking about your baby. So don't be embarrassed about it.

That said... babies are a teensy, weensy bit boring. Not yours, yours is well amazing. But everyone needs someone to talk to. Being at home with a baby can be isolating, the rest of the world is carrying on like nothing happened while you're at home worrying if watching Cersei Lannister bang her brother will psychologically damage a three-week-old.

If you are going to really enjoy yourself at home with your baby you need to make friends – someone to point out when there is poo smeared on your jeans, someone who has baby wipes handy and can help clean it up, someone who probably has poo smeared on their own jeans. I'm talking about other mums. Although befriending random strangers with shit-smeared jeans would also make for a very interesting maternity leave.

Drinking coffee whilst discovering that someone else has had an equally bad night as you is exactly what you need when you have a baby. Not that I like to revel in other people's suffering but it's just nice to know that you're not doing it alone. Even though a lot of the time you are alone, apart from the baby who I keep forgetting about because babies don't really count as company unless you're used to having conversations where the other person only communicates through squelchy bum noises or angry screaming.

In real life, friendships develop over time through shared experiences; you meet people at work, at school, at a party. One night you gatecrash the Christmas party of a cool internet startup together and accidentally fall into the Christmas tree; you tell her the guy she's split up with is a worthless dick; two years later you're giving a speech at their wedding where you mention the Christmas tree incident and gloss over the fact that you think the Groom is still a dick; eventually one day you throw up in her favourite handbag and she doesn't kill you. That's how friends are made.

Baby friendships are not like this. You make friends with people because they have a child roughly the same age as yours and you are both worried about your vaginas. There's no deciding if you like them, or working out if you have things in common. You *don't need to like them* and you have a baby in common.

Baby friendships bypass all those years of female bonding, fast forwarding straight to the bit where you compare cracked nipples whilst sobbing on the sofa. In real life, if someone you had met for coffee just once rocked up at your house, cried for half an hour, talked about her fanny and brought round a friend who screamed and vomited all over your best cushion, alarm bells might start ringing but this is pretty much the ideal start for a baby friendship. Remember, if they can cry and puke round your house you can do the same around theirs. Oh, and no one sane keeps 'best cushions' and small children in the same house.

It turns out that having a baby the same age as yours can be all you need to maintain a friendship in those early stages. Do not underestimate the power of this shared experience. Pregnancy, childbirth and parenting a new-born are all intense experiences, you don't need to have other things in common for tapping into this support network.

Think of it this way: when you start a new job it's important to at least try and get on with your colleagues even if you don't envisage inviting them to your wedding. In turn, other mums will help you negotiate motherhood in those early stages; if you're lucky you can learn from their mistakes and if you're out of luck let them learn from yours. In two years' time you might still be BFF's or maybe you'll just remain friends on Facebook just like any other group of colleagues.

So where do you meet all these new mums? I met one good baby friend in leafy North London when she shouted across the street at me: 'Hey there! I'm pregnant too! Do you want to come round my house?' This is an ideal way to build a support network although it only really works in urban areas. You could spend a long time stood in the road in rural Yorkshire waiting for pregnant women to walk past your house. If standing in the street shouting at passers by isn't for you then you need to go join some baby groups or head to the park. (Aha! the street thing doesn't sound so bad now does it?)

Let me be clear, even though new mum friendships are built in a different way to traditional friendships it is still scary starting them. If befriending complete strangers in the park still gives you the fear then remember your secret weapon – y'know the one in the pram with the cute smile. Babies are amazing icebreakers, they should hand them out at corporate networking events. Try to remember the last time you did something that frightened you, something where you had to dig deep into your personal strength, like, I dunno, having a baby!

Talking to a complete stranger is not even on the same level as having a baby, if you can do that – you can do this; just remember most new mums are just as scared of you as you are of them. Or have I got mothers confused with lions again?

Here is a list of things you could say to ladies in the park to tempt them back to yours.

1. Do you know any good baby groups locally?

2. How old is your baby?

3. I have literally no fucking clue what I'm doing, please come round my house for biscuits which I don't have because I ate them all whilst crying on the toilet this morning.

Any of these are completely acceptable opening gambits.

Hopefully, once you get into the swing of things, you will have coffee dates with lots of mums because making baby friends is basically like internet dating but without all the disappointing sex. This is definitely a numbers game, you're not necessarily looking for 'the one' just 'the one who lives in the same geographical area who is free to meet during the day and isn't an absolute twat'. Think Tinder rather than Guardian Soulmates and swipe right to everyone.

It's good to meet mums with a mix of opinions, mums who do things differently to you, mums who do things you perhaps wouldn't do. Watching a mix of parenting styles in action is a brilliant way to learn that whatever choices you make, there is no one way to raise a child. If you're only hanging out with people who think the same as you, it's easy to start thinking your way is the 'right' way when really, there is no 'right' way to parent. The sooner you work this out, the easier life as a mum becomes.

Remember parenting is not a competitive sport, babies learn to sit up, roll over, walk, talk and use the toilet all at different times and there are no prizes for being the first. As a new mum, it's all too easy to feel judged or as though you are failing. Try not to judge other mums and their choices and it's easier to feel confident about yourself. Invest some time in building a supportive network and you will get the best out of your maternity leave. It's important to be surrounded by friends who make you feel happy about the choices you're making as a parent. Apart from one, you should always have one friend who's a complete bitch just to keep life interesting.

While you're assembling a crack commando unit of kick-ass mums, don't panic if you feel you're losing touch with old friends who don't have young children. This is natural while you are both busy with very different lives. You're free during the day while old friends are at work. You are busy in the evenings trying to work out why your baby refuses to go to sleep while they're out 'having a life'.

Back in the real world, people still meet up for coffee and a chat, mums with babies know that sometimes you will meet up and not exchange a single meaningful word. The entire time you spend together will be spent jiggling and shushing and shovelling nipples in and out of horrible bras. Your old friends want to meet up in wildly impossible places where they serve afternoon tea in vintage mismatched china and there are no change facilities or space for a pram.

'Hey cute cafe owners! Here's a thought why not stop messing around setting timers for a cup of tea and find me somewhere to wipe my baby's arse?'

So try not to feel too left out when all your old pals head off on a girly spa weekend and you're left at home reading their updates on Facebook whilst doing the night shift. Your time will come round again - you'll be back embarrassing yourself on social media before you know it.

The important message when you become a mother is *be kind to others* and *be kind to yourself* and remember just because the other mums look boring doesn't mean they are.

Most new mothers are very much into the 'doing sensible grown up shit' part of life. Of course, all the women at playgroup look boring... they're at a baby group! No one gatecrashes Baby Sing & Sign pissed on tequila shots and starts chanting Strip! Strip! Strip! when the vicar pops in for a custard cream. But that doesn't mean there aren't people there who wouldn't have at least thought about doing this in a previous life.

Now you've got your team let's have some fun...

Chapter 6
I am never, ever going to playgroup. Ever.

If you are going to survive being at home with a baby, you need to be *away from* home with a baby as much as you possibly can. Don't panic! I'm not talking about getting rid of the baby… I'm talking about getting out of the house. There are many good reasons for this – babies make an inordinate amount of mess and they are never up-to-date on the latest *Made In Chelsea* gossip but the main reason you need to attempt to leave the house at least once a day is because being at home will drive you fucking crackers.

When you are at work, all you dream about is spending time at home; you live for those long lie-ins at the weekend, fantasizing about the next bank holiday. The feeling of release and relaxation that comes with spending time at home lasts for about four days, that's without the baby, with the baby there's no sense of freedom and relaxation, there's just you. At home. With a baby.

Don't get me wrong, babies are wonderful bringers of joy, lighting up the lives of all who come into contact with them, but they can also cry and poo a lot and as a mum it's nice to have them crying and pooing in someone else's place for at least some of the time. Even if you love your home, it's amazing how quickly you can get sick of staring at the same four walls. Remember, you're not just seeing them all day, often you will spend all night staring at them too.

Once you've had a bit of time to master the general looking-after-a-baby-at-home stuff, it's time to start going out. The first time you go outside alone with your baby can be quite stressful. You will take *a lot* of shit with you. I think I took about 17 nappies and three changes of clothes on a five minute walk to the corner shop for milk.

You need a lot of strength to haul the stuff you think you need when you first go out. In reality, you don't actually *need* the bags and bags of stuff but if they make you feel better, why not?

When our daughter was about 10 months old, my partner took her to the park but left the all-important bag of stuff at home. My Saturday morning 'me time' was ruined as I paced the house in abject panic stressing about how on earth the two of them would cope out on the mean streets of Highgate with no organic rice cakes to hand.

'Mum he's gone out to the park without baby wipes and fluffy rabbit! How long before I should call the police?'

Once I'd calmed down I sat back and started fantasizing about how smug I could be when he returned home a shattered man, sobbing at the horrific time he'd endured, which was actually way more fun than a morning watching *Saturday Kitchen* and painting my toenails, if you can imagine such things.

He returned having borrowed a nappy and wipes off the other mums in the park. Not only had I experienced a morning alone feeling smug, he had made all the other mums in the park feel superior when they got to laugh at stupid Daddy forgetting the change bag. Sometimes I forget the father of my children is probably the greatest person I've ever met.

After this epiphany I was able to skip, gaily out of the house with just a smartphone and devil may care attitude.[3] And you will get there too once you master the key rules of getting out and about with a small baby in tow, namely:

1. Take the baby with you everywhere you go.

2. Don't forget to bring the baby back home with you.

I think that's it.

Basically as long as you don't leave the baby at home unattended, or on the No72 bus you've nailed it.

Once you're out there going places, and doing stuff, you realise the world with a baby and a pram is different to the world you knew before and the biggest cultural shock you're in for is this: life moves at a different pace outside of rush hour and office lunchtimes.

At work, you interact with the world around you with urgency. You nip out at lunchtime to grab a sandwich, you shout your order to baristas as soon as you step in the door of a cafe, you make your way home via the shortest distance possible, grabbing the best seat on the bus or train so you can trim five seconds off your commute. You're surrounded by busy people going places quickly, living life at breakneck speed.

But cast your mind back to that time you had a Doctor's appointment and you were still sat in the waiting room 20 minutes after your allotted time and you got really angry with the surgery receptionist because you had work to get back to and she just shrugged like you had nothing better to do than sit there waiting and waiting and you were definitely going to write a letter of complaint to your MP but then life

---

[3] This is a bare faced lie, I have never left the house with less than two bags, I just wanted to check and see if anyone is actually paying attention to these footnotes.

happened and you never did? Well that is how the rest of the world works *all the fucking time.*

People think that slow service is something exotic, something that happens on holiday in the sunshine. Well it's not, it happens here, at home, when everyone is at work. On maternity leave there is a complete lack of urgency everywhere you go – as though the whole world is basically letting you know that they know you have nowhere else to be. Which you don't because the only place you need to be is with your baby.

And that's fine. Being with your baby is your job now but it does make you feel a teeny, weeny bit unimportant; another chipping away of the person you once were. Try not to let it get you down, the rest of the world can ignore you and keep you waiting but you will always be the most important thing in the world to your baby even if you do have to spend a lot of time together in crappy waiting rooms.

Becoming a mum for the first time will also redefine your attitude to being late. I was always taught that being late is rude, it shows that you don't respect the person you are late to meet. Being late with a baby is pretty much a given so try not to get too upset about it – whether you're the one who is late, or the person left waiting. I don't care how organised you were in your career. When you become a mum, that military attention to detail needs to drop off for sanity's sake. Even if you do maintain a level of pre baby organisation you will never make it out of the house on time, every time, and really what's the rush? All your new friends will be running late too because new mums are incredibly flaky.

Yet another reason why you can never have too many baby friends. Take a group of 10 women with new-born babies and one of them will have been up all night, one will have a baby that is ill, and five of them will just be leaving the house when their babies do a massive shit. (Someone should really do some research into the effect stepping out of the front door has on a small baby's bowel. If you're ever worried about a baby not pooing simply make an important date and try getting ready on time; guaranteed just as you leave: Kaboom!)

Anyway, now you have a baby it's perfectly acceptable to be late because you're meeting at the cafe in the park not the latest pop up bar where 'the Ceviche is to die for', so when you do get stood up you don't *look* like someone who got stood up because: baby.

Going anywhere with a group of baby friends can be logistically challenging. Simply walking and trying to hold a conversation whilst each pushing a pram is impossible – pavements simply aren't designed for this. You will have to perfect the art of all walking in a long line shouting at the person three prams behind you. It's not uncommon to see chain gangs of new mums parading through town shouting 'How's your bumhole doing now, Trish?'

If you ever want to catch a bus together, you can forget it. If a bus driver ever says to you, 'You'll have to fold it up love!' run away. Fast. Ultra marathon runners would crumble at the challenge of collapsing a pram, whilst holding a baby on a moving bus. Not to worry. You can always wait for the next bus which may or may not have space for you. You're not in a rush are you?

Just pushing a pram can also throw up lots of physical challenges. For the first year, every time I walked into a shop I announced my arrival by ramming the pram into the door and swearing under my breath. Not an ideal first impression.

But over time I got better at going out with a baby, starting with basic skills like getting through swing doors with a pram and progressing onto more advanced tricks like dealing with a poosplosion[4] using those tiny napkins they have in coffee shops until one day you will be able to push a pram laden down with bottles of wine with one hand whilst carrying a hot coffee in the other and not even swearing.

Having a baby will make you see your local area in a completely different light. Where once there were not enough cool places to hang out after work, now there are not enough child-friendly spots to hang out in during the day. As a parent, top of your shortlist will be anywhere that has space to get a pram through the door – you'll be surprised at how many spots are off limits for this reason. Only once you're through the door can you assess if a place is 'child friendly'.

Child friendly is open to wide interpretation; the most basic being *'we have a high chair'* or *'staffed by teenagers who couldn't give a shit what you do'* right through to places that have clean floors and changing facilities. Clean floors are a huge selling point when your baby starts crawling.

Proper child-friendly places don't necessarily have boxes of toys or high chairs, they have staff who are friendly to children. I know, crazy huh! Sympathetic staff who will smile at you pityingly when your baby screams and shits and won't ask you to go breastfeed in a manky toilet.

Whilst hunting for baby-friendly parts of town, you will find all sorts of wonderful new places you never knew existed some good (baby rooms and secret lifts in shops) and some bad (like having to push your pram three miles out of the way to get to a ramped access round the back of the building next to the stinky bins).

---

[4] poosplosion: an output from a tiny baby's bottom of such immense force and size that it explodes out of the nappy, up the back and onto your baby's head. See also Poonami, nappy buster.

This wonderful introduction into the world of babies and prams is basically just setting you up for this: the best places to hang out with all your new mum friends are baby groups.

I'm sorry. I know it sounds dreadful. Before I had a baby, the thought of hanging out at baby groups, filled with a load of mums comparing sleep patterns, sounded like torture. Once I had a baby, it didn't sound any more attractive. But honestly they do help.

Let's start by making one thing clear. No one wants to go to playgroup. No sane adult wakes up in the morning after a disturbed night's sleep and thinks.

What I really fancy doing today is sitting in an overheated church hall next to a massive pile of germ-infested snot-covered toys, drinking stewed tea, and watching other people's children have a meltdown over a packet of value malted milk biscuits. That would just elevate my day into awesome.'

No one. Not even the women who were really, really into babies before they had them. Mums (and Dads) go to playgroup because this is what passes for 'going out' once you have a baby.

This is such a totally fucked up concept it's pointless even trying to get your head around it before the baby comes, but you will at some point find yourself dragging a screaming toddler out of the house to go to Baby Boogie even though the very thought of jumping around at the leisure centre to a horrendous shitty rock guitar version of *The Wheels On The Bus* makes you want to cry.

How on earth can this happen? you ask.

Because it's something to do. It's somewhere to go with your child that you don't have to stress about; baby groups are safe and easy places to hang out, where you know you won't have to apologise if your child makes a terrible noise or an appalling smell.

Surprisingly, no one puts this on their promotional material:

'Book now for Muzik Totz. What else are you going to do Thursday morning?' or *'Muzik Totz provides a nurturing space for mums to check their smartphones while their babies roll around on the floor and crap themselves'.*

Instead, they concentrate on the developmental benefits of their classes quoting research that children who study dance before they can actually walk properly all grow up to be Nobel prize winning scientists with perfect teeth.

As a first time mum, the sheer array of classes and sessions is overwhelming so here is a guide to the most basic options.

Baby Classes. Expensive excuses for new mums to hang round and make friends because apparently it's frowned upon to spend *every* morning in the pub with a baby. There are sessions for music, sensory play, signing, foreign languages, massage, yoga, and swimming.

On top of sleepless nights and the stress of *'Is my baby feeding/breathing correctly?'* parents can now also worry that their child will be the only one that can't sing a pitch perfect Frère Jacques whilst executing a downward facing dog. Baby massage did teach me how to pick up a baby that's been basted in vegetable oil (carefully) and through Baby Yoga I discovered how, if you are on all fours doing cat pose for too long, a small child will incorporate you into their train track. Usually as a bridge, but once as a station. I'd rather not go into any more detail about that.

Toddler Lessons. Often you will get one session free, this is because small children LOVE doing something for the first time. Once they've enjoyed the taster session, and you've paid for a full term of tennis classes, children tend to change their minds and you will both spend the next five Tuesday mornings wishing you had ignored your inner Judy Murray and stayed at home watching telly and eating biscuits.

The Park. Big green space full of flirting teenagers, happy-go-lucky dog owners, and carefree office workers sunbathing and picnicking at lunch. This is not for you. Your bit is over there, in the corner, where all the screams are coming from. Move along.

Playground. Aka 'The swings'. Don't expect to relax – you will be far too busy pulling scabby plasters and half-chewed crisp packets out of your child's mouth as they munch their way through the sand pit. Playgrounds are even worse when it's cold as the UK is not really a standing-around-outside kinda place. As an adult you will spend most of your time trying to defrost your hands in your pockets whilst watching a 2-year-old faceplant off a spinny roundy thing.

Soft Play. Imagine a playground that someone has covered in brightly coloured bubble wrap and thrown a big net over before moving it indoors. Add in some discarded socks, weird sticky patches, a smell of puke and special corners where seven years of dust can collect.

Finally, throw in some giant foam rollers and tunnels for adult sized humans to get stuck in and a plastic slide so fast everyone over 18 shouts SHIIIIT! the first time they use it.[5] That is Soft Play.

Playgroup. Traditionally a playgroup will have two sections – one for babies and one for toddlers. The toddler area is the one where all the mums are on their smartphones while a massive fight ensues over a germ-encrusted ride-on police car.

The baby area will have mats and cushions on the floor in case anyone collapses with sleep exhaustion. Allow yourself 45 minutes to leave at the end as everyone tries to locate their pram in the 'buggy park' and ram it through a heavy swing door without hitting a child in the face.

---

[5] Okay, maybe not *everyone*.

Stay & Play. This is where you take your child to play but have to stay with them. Exactly like a playgroup… but also totally different. If someone has gone to the trouble of calling a session 'Stay and Play' you will be very much expected to do both the staying *and* the playing. Sitting on a chair live tweeting the awesome tantrum you're witnessing is generally frowned upon. You are going to be on the floor 'engaging with your child' whilst pretending that you do this kind of stuff all the time at home.

Attractions. Hideously expensive things marketed as a *'Fun day out for all the family!'* The reality is that they are always at least an hour too far away in the car and once you arrive none of the rides are suitable.

Once you've got into a weekly routine of playgroup, parks and singing sessions in the church hall, life starts to feel a little better but even these activities after a while can start to get a little… repetitive. After several months of doing the same baby-related stuff you may find yourself starting to feel… ummm what's the word? Bored. Out of your tiny mind.

About the same time you start to get bored – your baby starts to move. Crawling babies are hard work, they refuse to sit nicely in their prams and be pushed around to places mummy wants to visit but they can't walk anywhere and still require you to bring along prams, change bags, snacks and toys.

So you are faced with a dilemma, a very particular first world problem but a problem all the same. Stick or twist? Do you stick with what you know or head off out somewhere new for the day? If the very thought of gluing feathers onto yet another cardboard tiara at Busy Bees Krafty Korner makes your heart sink, it might be time to pack up your nappies and head out somewhere new. Somewhere exciting, somewhere that's not all about babies. I've seen these places, they exist, and – what's more – some of them are near shops so you can go shopping if your baby falls asleep. Honestly it's true I once managed to purchase a whole new jumper from All Saints doing this.

Before you get too excited, we're not talking about going white water rafting or to cocktail-making classes, I'm thinking more along the lines of an art gallery or a zoo. Also it won't be easy, there will be tears from either you or the baby but sometimes you need a trip into the real world to make you feel like a person again and not just a mum.

In order to go anywhere new, you are going to have to get there. Travelling with small children, either by car or on public transport should be approached in the same way you would childbirth – prepare for the worst, pack lots of food and when it gets too much scream for help!

The places I loved the most were museums and art galleries. Okay, let's get this clear, your baby will have absolutely no interest in whatever exhibition is on so don't worry about that. But galleries and museums often have lovely big clean (ish) floors to roll around on plus they have toilets, cafes and baby changing facilities and – one for the toddlers here – lifts and interesting floor grates.

When my children were toddlers they both adored shoving rice cakes through Victorian cast iron floor grates; it was one of the best things ever. Add to that the pure unbridled joy of riding up and down in a lift and they were in seventh heaven at any museum without even having to look at what was actually displayed. In London, we visited The Natural History Museum, The British Museum, The National Gallery, Tate Modern and The Hayward Gallery. Apart from the David Shrigley exhibition I don't think there was a single exhibition that ever interested a two-year-old and a baby but for me it was worth all the battling on public transport just to go and stand somewhere new every once in a while and look at something beautiful that didn't want me to change it's nappy.

Often museums and galleries will have small areas for children – the kind of thing you would think looked rubbish before you had a baby. Rest assured, however, that hitting a button and making part of a map light up can entertain a small child for an entire 15 minutes.

I found the 'less attractive to other visitors' the place was, the better it was to visit with babies. I thought The Natural History Museum would be amazing but actually it was always just a bit too busy – if it's not packed in school holidays it's packed with school trips – damn other people's children! However the more obscure galleries of the V & A, we could wander in peace while my daughter shouted at statues Lion! Lady! Lion! Lady! for hours.

You can also find some fantastic baby name inspiration in museums and art galleries – I really fell for the name Decimus until I discovered it meant tenth child at which point I went straight off it.

Zoos and farms are also great places for a day out but they aren't always suitable for crawlers, in fact if your baby is keen to be on the move a farm is the worst place to go, even I draw the line at watching my children crawl through cow muck. If there's a nice grassy bit you're okay but often these places involve a lot of lifting children up to look in pens. Avoid if you are heavily pregnant with number two.

There are plenty of fun things to do with your baby if you're brave enough; it's up to you to find the things which you find least distressing. You can book your baby in for baby gymnastics and beginners French classes or you can take them to playgroup and watch your offspring stick their fingers in your friends' children's noses. Both are equally fantastic ways to occupy babies. Neither of them will teach a baby to speak French. I did everything with baby number one – swimming, singing, and baby yoga classes. And nada with baby number two. I don't feel at all bad about this because doing stuff with small children is as much about keeping Mummy happy and occupied as it is the baby.

Chapter 7
Modern mum problems: Stuff your mum never had to worry about

Everyone likes to romanticize life gone by and it's no different with parenting.

Apparently, previous generations just got on with it, things were easier, and there was less 'fuss'. Maybe life was better in the old days, when you could leave your baby outside in a pram for most of the morning and afternoon, but how the hell did my mum manage with cloth nappies, no hummus, and children's telly that was only on for two hours a day?

Today we have pesto, 24-hour Peppa Pig, and instant access to the Internet everywhere we go so we can read Buzzfeed lists telling us how everything was great in life when we were young and how it's all shit now. This nostalgia for the old days has been going forever.

11 things only people who grew up in the Palaeolithic Era will understand.

1. You were on the Paleo diet before it got faddy.

2. No one bothered with stair gates – you lived in a cave!

3. Your best friend was a woolly mammoth.

4. Until your parents killed and ate him with a rock.

5. After that your best friend was a rock.

6. No one cared if you threw your dinner on the floor
   – you lived in a cave!

7. Fire was a life saver not a health and safety risk.

8. You were actively encouraged to paint on the walls
   – you lived in a cave!

9. Your dad invented rafts.

10. You were breastfed for years and no one thought it
    was weird.

11. You lived in a cave!

The biggest way parenting has changed over the time is right here in your hands. Yes, this bloody book. I have a book on running a household from 1947 and there are just 30 pages about having a baby, starting with the ideal floorplan for a nursery, how much a baby should sleep, advice on breastfeeding, budgeting and suitable toys, and not one single sentence about pregnancy.

Today the amount of information you are expected to process, whilst walking around as the size of a house, is enormous. You can't get your shoes on when heavily pregnant so you have to stay home and read research papers about vitamin D deficiency in children. The next evolutionary step for the human race will probably be a two-year gestation period so expectant mothers have time to absorb all the information they are expected to know.

Parenting advice is everywhere – leaflets, blogs, websites, magazines and books. Our parents never had to deal with all this. None of the experts agree and accepted best practice can change in a short space of time!

You can spend ages researching a decision about how you will raise a baby you haven't yet had and then flippin' science goes and discovers that the path you were about to go down is now proven to cause childhood obesity and nasal warts. Which should make you feel safer because you've avoided having an obese, warty-nosed child but which actually just makes you feel sad that you've got to start thinking all over again.

The government tries to help by creating easily digestible leaflets with lots of pictures so everyone can understand them. Terrifying pamphlets with illustrations of babies licking plug sockets, playing with boiled kettles, and choking on peanuts.

Not letting your baby play with boiled kettles or plug sockets is pretty much *exactly* what you were planning on doing anyway so all this information does is push new parents into a state of high alert, panicking about their baby being in the same room as a freshly-boiled kettle.

'Get out! Get out! Take the baby! Save yourselves! I'm making a pot of Earl Grey!'

I was so worried about being locked out of the house when making trips to the outside bin with smelly nappies that I stopped going out of the front door, instead leaving bags of stinking nappies piled outside the front doorstep like a warning sign for canvassers. Beware, crazy first-time mum lives here!

To make things easier for new parents, lots of lovely companies have spotted this first time parent panic and decided to help out by developing expensive new things you didn't know you needed until you had a baby. At a time when finances are already tight, you will start researching costly non-toxic paints and safe-to-touch kettles. Ironic really, when what new parents actually need is five minutes peace with a hot cup of tea.

Obviously, you should read all the information but try not to let it add to your big list of things to worry about. Don't let yourself get too stressed about whether your baby has had enough tummy time or is latching on correctly and concentrate your efforts on something that will help: Crap TV.

This is not a joke. Ask any mum and they'll all tell you that screaming warnings at Spencer's latest conquest on *Made In Chelsea*, binge watching all six seasons of *Gossip Girl* or seeing someone burn their biscuits on *The Great British Bake Off* will help you be a better parent.

'Research time' is also another period when your new mum friends will prove invaluable. Share the reading list between yourselves and compare notes. Just remember not to make too many firm decisions before the baby arrives. Maybe your baby will love the sleep routine you've got mapped out for them, perhaps you'll express bottles full of breast milk, but *don't* beat yourself up if your choices have to be modified or binned completely.

On top of the information overload, there's the challenge of navigating social media as a new mum. How on earth did people cope before Facebook? Can you imagine not knowing that Julie – who used to sit two desks down from you – had been on a girls' weekend in Dublin? You remember Julie. Yes you do. She was blonde. Or was she a redhead? Broke her leg that time? Oh, that was Helen wasn't it. Who the fuck is Julie then?

Social media is perfect reading when you're at home with a baby. Twitter, Facebook and Instagram all present bite-sized chunks of information that are perfect for the sleep-deprived brain of a new mum. You have no actual time to sit down and read a book, every time you open a newspaper it makes you cry and magazines are full of clothes you can no longer afford, fit into, or have any occasion to wear. But a quick scan of Twitter and you're pretty much up to date.

You wouldn't make for a great interview on *Newsnight* but you could probably wing it on *Loose Women*.

The big problem with social media is that it's all too easy to compare the lives of other people to your own and come up wanting. Working in television was never glamorous – most location shoots involve standing in a cold empty building freezing your tits off at ungodly hours of the morning making inane chit chat with the onscreen 'talent' whilst waiting for a runner to return with a can of WD40. I understood this, I lived it. But when I was stuck at home with a baby, all my former colleagues seemed to be swanning around at the BAFTA's, hanging out with celebrities in LA hotels, or posting selfies of themselves with the Chuckle Brothers. And I felt left out and left behind.

It wasn't just the big things that got me, complaining about a new film release being rubbish, or a passenger who smelled on the train was just as likely to make me feel left out as *'Hey Facebook! Hit me up with your suggestions for boutique hotels in New York!'* At a time when you are outside your comfort zone, feeling a little unsure of your place in the world, and worried your career is going to nosedive, you have a window into the lives of everyone else you've ever known and they are all having a better time than you.

They are not. It just looks that way on Facebook. Remember the first rule of Instagram. If you zoom in really close and whack a filter on it... *everything* in life can look better. Apart from your face.

Once you become a parent you don't stop wanting all the things you wanted before, you just know that they are not quite as important as keeping your baby alive and loved. So try to hold on to that and don't get caught up comparing your life to other people's.

Social Media Etiquette for Babies. Sharing pictures and news of your baby online is a brilliant way of keeping in touch with ~~people you can't really be bothered to speak to~~ relatives who live far away. If you're worried about posting too many pictures of your baby on Facebook just remember the golden rule.

Everyone likes babies. But not as much as they like cats.

Think about it. Your friend posts a picture of a cross-eyed baby in an elf sleep suit, everyone 'likes' it. So far so meh. Your friend posts the same picture with a cat in the sleep suit. That shit is going viral.

A birth announcement on Social Media should be short and to the point explaining what it is, how much it weighs and what it will be called. Ideally the Father should post the announcement because ~~it's about time he did something~~ the new mother will be tired and emotional. If I had been let loose on Facebook after giving birth I would have posted something like this:

I have a baby! It's a boy... or a girl, one of the two. I don't remember much after the bit where I thought I was going to die. It's got a head – a big fuck off head – I remember that. Everything anyone ever told me about giving birth was total bollocks. I'm off to pop more pills now. Tatty Bye.

You may include a photo but if you want to save time just use one of your friend's pictures – no one will notice – new born babies all look the same anyway. Unlike cats.

On no account should any gory details of the birth be included. If you have plans to eat the placenta, keep them to yourselves. Unless they involve a cat in which case the world needs to know.

Once the baby is home you will want to share his or hers many firsts. Always remember the baby/cat rule and ask yourself the question before posting: *'Is this photo of my precious firstborn as good as a picture of a cross-eyed cat dressed up as an elf?'*

Finally, if you're fed up of seeing your Facebook timeline full of other people's baby photos why not get some new friends? Horrible, unpopular friends who won't attract members of the opposite sex and procreate. Better still get a cat.

Chapter 8
Where does
Daddy fit in?

The problem with writing about the differences between Mummy and Daddy is that you find yourself having to write the words Mummy and Daddy a lot. If you are reading this before you have started a family this may make you feel a bit uneasy. *We're never going to call each other Mummy and Daddy all the time. It's weird!*

Yes. Yes, it is. But unfortunately you literally cannot stop it from happening. At first you do it because it's new and cute. *What does Mummy want to do today? Does Daddy want a cup of tea?* But then you realise you can't stop it even though you now both find it even more strange and creepy than you did before. Eventually you can't remember what you used to call each other before you became parents or how you ever managed to argue without a baby in the middle to pass on the message.

Maybe Daddy could get you dressed today as he hasn't been up half the night?

Perhaps Mummy will cheer up when Daddy's got you dressed? Oh snufflypig... who's got a grumpy Mummy!?!

If you think that sounds awful, wait until one of you calls the other Mummy or Daddy when you are having sex. Nature's contraceptive. Hey ho, cheer up Mummy! Time to find out how things with Daddy are going to change beyond all recognition.

* * * * *

There's nothing like putting your womb through its paces to make you realise what a wonderful creation women are. Men are great at lots of things but as far as actual production of people goes, it's embarrassing. I've done a very unscientific study and realised that almost everyone I know was created by a person of the female persuasion. Men it seems are too busy arguing about *Top Gear*, and not looking for things properly, to be pregnant.

After putting in all the hard work with pregnancy and all the giving birth shenanigans, cuddling your baby feels like proper recompense. As a new mum you'll be keen to get to grips with all the tasks you need to learn; your baby basically just wants to snuggle with you, or your boob at least, which leaves Daddy standing there like a spare part making naff jokes about how your boobs used to be just for him. Why do they feel the need to do this?

In the early days, it can be hard to let other people look after your baby because new-born babies are super cuddly and after being pregnant for forever it's nice to be able to do stuff. No matter how exhausted you are, it's amazing how you can still want to go and comfort your own baby when they wake you up for the 17th time in the night.

The problems arise further down the line when you realise Mummy has been doing everything for baby, and Daddy hasn't got a clue where to start. Not because your relationship is like something from the 1950's, or because Daddy is useless, but because it was simply easier for Mummy to do it, and you liked doing it. Also, you were both exhausted by the whole not sleeping properly thing and it just kind of happened. One day you woke up and realised there was a four-month-old baby boy in the house who had only ever gone wee wee directly into his mother's face.

Make sure you both have the chance to practice being Mummy and Daddy right from the start, this is important for lots of reasons but the big fat selfish one is this – *at some point, later on, Mummy will need to get her hair trimmed.*

Other books might witter on about father/ baby bonding, equal parenting, and all that shizzle but I'm thinking of your split ends. As a first time mum, you might think you don't ever need to leave your baby's side but you will at some point want to have some time on your own. Really, you will. Otherwise, you will end up as the new mum who can't go out for a drink with her friends because 'no one else can settle the baby' and then you might as well give up hope.

So suck it up in the early days and let Daddy get stuck in. Bugger off and leave them alone, you need to give your partner space to look after his baby, his way. This will probably be the wrong way, but just let him get on with it; no hovering around in the background telling him he's using the wrong coloured muslin or pointing out that his version of *The Wheels on the Bus* is sexist.

Zip it Mummy!

Try to remember just how annoying it is when people tell you you're doing stuff wrong and keep your trap shut when he uses a whole packet of baby wipes on just one wet nappy.

With any luck you'll end up in the horribly frustrating situation where despite you being the person who has put their career on hold to stay at home and look after the children full-time, your partner is *just as good at it.* I mean, obviously, this is a brilliant situation to be in but at the same time it would be nice if the kids thought it was slightly less fun when Daddy is in charge. Maybe I'm being mean but I think I'd actually feel better if I came home and at least one member of my family was crying and lamenting what a terrible time they'd had. Daddy or the children, I'm not fussy.

One thing people don't often talk about, is how hard it can be to leave your baby for the first time. After having them sit on your bladder for nine months, and then carrying them in your arms most of the day, the first time you go out without your new companion is a truly weird experience. It feels very odd, as though you have forgotten something very important, as if part of you is missing. A bit like leaving the house without your mobile phone if leaving your mobile phone behind could make your boobs swell with milk.

My daughter was about six-weeks-old when my partner suggested I 'nip into town' while he watched the baby. I did not want to 'nip into town' on my own. I was scared. What of? I have no idea. Mainly I think I was worried about missing out. Fear of missing out – FOMO – is something most modern women are used to, but usually it's reserved for big parties or fun weekends away with the girls; this time I was worried I might miss a particularly cute gurgle or a massive wet nappy. What if she started doing some amazing new thing whilst I was out and I missed it? I would probably be vilified by the national press.

'Evil mum misses daughter's first smile while out shopping for new toothbrush, child likely to be psychologically damaged by this appalling event.'

Okay, maybe I was being slightly overdramatic about leaving my baby for the first time but I genuinely did not feel comfortable about it. We were getting along fine, but what if she decided she liked being without me? She had been near me for every single second of her perfect life and now I was abandoning her to go shopping for stuff I didn't really even need. I could probably manage without deodorant until she started school.

I went out to have some time to myself even though I really did not want to spend any time with myself. I am always with myself and I find myself incredibly dull company. I much prefer hanging out with other people who can distract me from my own boring self. Unfortunately, all my friends were busy doing exciting stuff so I went out on my own for the first time as a fully-fledged mum.

Everything felt weird without a baby slowing me down; my boobs were having a terrible time of it too, all lumpy and angry. I got off the train at Camden Town because I thought I was going to throw up. Either that, or my boobs were going to explode. Surprisingly the first bodily fluid I emitted was not breast milk or vomit but tears. If you are going to stand in the middle of the street, sobbing, then Camden is as good a place as any... a kind man loitering round the tube station gave me a tissue. I went for a coffee and called my partner 'just to check' then ran around Boots The Chemist bulk-buying supplies so I never had to leave the house again.

Writing this down, I realise this is not a funny story about the reality of parenting; it's a tragic story about a grown woman crying in the street like a total loser while a man who may (or may not) have been selling drugs offered her a tissue and some ketamine (thinking about it now he was *definitely* selling drugs). But the more I've spoken about this, the more I realise most mums feel this way. It's normal to be a bit stressed about leaving your baby with someone else, even when that someone else is the baby's father.

If your first trip out alone, in the day, is a disaster – don't worry... this will all be eclipsed when you have your first night out drinking without your baby. (Just to clarify there is no night out drinking *with* your baby, babies are notoriously bad at paying for their round which is why they have been banned from most licenced premises.)

Your first night out with the girls, post-baby, will redefine your whole understanding of social embarrassment. *Leave your smartphone at home* as you do not want to be anywhere near social media when you are drunk without your baby. What starts as going out for 'a few drinks to catch up with old friends' will end up with you getting absolutely arseholed, imploring your mates to all have a baby immediately, offering to show the hot bearded bartender your stitches, and then being carried home in tears. All this after just one small glass of wine.

Nothing you say on this first night out will persuade anyone who doesn't have children to give it a try. They should play videos of mummy's first night out to school children. It would slash teenage pregnancy rates. And the best bit is still to come.

If your first night out is traumatic, wait until the next morning and you experience your first post-baby hangover. Remember how bad you felt after you left your baby to go to the shops? This is like that, but turned all the way up to 11. Your first hangover as a mum is a spectacular cycle of depression and self-loathing. I remember thinking mums do not throw up in the cutlery drawer and have to be forcibly stopped from breastfeeding. But the truth is mums *do* do things like this, although thankfully not as often as they used to... which is exactly the way it should be.

Obviously, if you're out every night, rolling around on the floor drunk, then something is definitely awry but cutting loose every now and again will absolutely help you to be a better mum. You just need to dig deep into your inner reserves to handle the horror of looking after a baby with a hangover. I don't care how momentous your hangovers have been in the past, nothing will compare with the ones you suffer while trying to look after your baby. You will spend the entire day feeling like a terrible, terrible person, trying to decipher the funny faces your perfect little angel is giving you. Was that a look of disgust or is there a poo brewing?

Remember that you're not a terrible person, you're doing your best, and that is probably just a poo brewing. Because guess what? Babies still require nappy changes when you're hungover. On a positive note, all this self-loathing is the perfect distraction – while you're busy dealing with the mummy guilt and the world's worst hangover, Daddy can be the one wiping piss out of his eyes for a change. Sorted.

After the initial shock of becoming parents together for the first time, our experiences as Mummy and Daddy started to diverge. By the time our daughter was one-year-old my partner's life was pretty much the same one he had pre-baby. In fact, I was surprised at how little his life had really changed. Sure, we were doing more family things on a weekend and he was pitching in at home, but during the week he was going to work and coming home just like before; his group of friends hadn't changed, his body was not completely unrecognisable, and he didn't seem to be losing confidence. Why would he?

This was in stark contrast to my life which was almost unrecognisable. Everything was different about me: what I did, who I did it with, where I hung out, how I looked, and how I felt. I'd got new friends, a new wardrobe of clothes I didn't even like, and having no 'proper job' to go to meant I was starting to lose some of my confidence. My old career was not very child-friendly; would I even be able to go back to work? What the hell would I wear for an interview if I did go back to work? Even more terrifyingly, what would I say? My conversational skills had been dulled and I had gained a nasty habit of shouting and pointing out 'interesting' things *Look! Bus! Cat! Interview Panel!*

As the gap widened between Mummy and Daddy our daughter became more of a handful, in the most brilliant, fantastic, but exhausting way.

When you are working full-time, the idea of being at home all day with no real structure to your day, hanging out with the person you adore most in the world, watching them learn to walk and talk and discover new things, sounds like heaven. Picnics in the park, afternoon naps, feeding the ducks. Bliss!

But lucky Mummy ignores all this because she is frazzled from spending all day having her face and boobs mauled. That picnic Daddy is fantasizing about probably does not involve wrestling fag ends, bottle tops and dog poo out of a baby's surprisingly powerful grip. The grass is always greener on the other side, even when it's full of fag ends and dog poo.

When you are at home with a baby, wearing vomit-stained jeans it's hard not to miss life at the office, sitting at a desk surrounded by pens – God, I miss pens. Having adult conversations about non-baby related things, wearing nice clothes and, best of all, not singing! A lunch break with no one sat on your lap sticking their fingers up your nose, conversations about, er, whatever people who aren't consumed with babies talk about... the commute! Getting on a bus instead of singing about conductors – a job that hasn't existed for 30 years now.

Meanwhile Daddy is actually at work. You remember work? Yeah, it was pretty annoying sometimes wasn't it? And quite tiring, doing stuff for other people when they want it, never getting a proper lunch hour, squishing up against other people's stinky armpits on the commute.

It's a tricky situation because *both* parents have been working all day. He thinks you can take it easy during the day, which you can't, while you think that he has had the commute home to relax, which he hasn't. And the baby thinks now is the perfect time to kick off, which it is not. So, six o'clock becomes a battleground.

In 'fantasy parenting world' Daddy opens the door, shouts 'I'm home!' and his beautiful family rush to the door showering him with cuddles and happy kisses. In the kitchen, dinner is on the table and everyone chats about how their day went while the baby gurgles happily in her highchair.

In reality Daddy walks towards the house with a sinking feeling as there are three messages on his phone all asking when he will be home, and a further two messages from when the baby has got hold of the phone and he can hear what is going on in the house (it does not sound good). He scales the mountain of nappy bags mummy has kindly left by the front door. In the kitchen, dinner is on the table, and the floor, and the walls. Basically there is nowhere in a five-foot radius of the baby that is not covered with dinner. The baby screams angrily in her highchair and Mummy bursts into tears. Welcome home dear!

There's no answer to this. Some days my partner would walk through the door, I would hand him his crying daughter and leave the room to go do my own crying in the other room. Neither of us would speak. When I think about this now, I realise that this is probably the most romantic thing that's ever happened. You can keep your candlelit dinners and mountain-top proposals, a man who will let you silently throw an angry baby at him is what you want.

Chapter 9
Stuff we don't talk about: Miscarriage

I cannot talk about pregnancy and having babies without talking about pregnancy loss.

I lost three pregnancies before I had my daughter and was third time lucky with my son. At the time losing a baby felt like it was a separate conversation to *having* a baby, when in reality it's all part of the journey. The part of the journey where you discover the train has been replaced by a crappy bus and it's going to take you twice as long to get where you're going and be four times more uncomfortable.

Even if you never suffer miscarriage personally, when you start hanging around with lots of ladies having babies, you will have friends who experience it. It's part of the story of starting a family for many people and it's a complete bastard. Personally for me it was a shitty, shitty time and I spent a lot of time being the designated crier at every girls' night out. Fortunately my friends are awesome and didn't mind me ruining the party for a whole two years; at least it made a change from me throwing up on their shoes.

During the great struggle to get pregnant and stay pregnant, I was very aware of other pregnant women, people who went on to have healthy, kicking babies while I was left with nothing but a pang of envy every time I saw their Facebook updates. There was a time when I remembered missed due dates, anniversaries of hospital visits, and soul crushing scans with fury. I hated watching pregnancy announcements in films or on television, some simpering pair of idiots gathering all their friends for dinner and making a big announcement, his hand laid protectively upon her belly. Even worse was the silly cow on screen who didn't even know she was pregnant – looking puzzled when she couldn't fasten her skinny jeans then throwing up in the toilet at work. *Crikey darling! I'm pregnant...*

As you can see my sisterly support was somewhat lacking during the great struggle to get pregnant and stay pregnant. I felt cheated of my moment by all the crushing false starts. Thank God, the trend for viral pregnancy announcements hadn't yet got going; I think I would have been hurling my laptop out of the window nearly every day.

Not to worry. I was not to be put off.

I attacked having a baby like another work project, reading, researching and forward planning and the more effort I put in, the worse the blow was when it came. I tried avoiding everything pregnant women are supposed to avoid – soft cheese, oysters and angry bears and I lost babies. So I decided to use reverse psychology on my own womb – ignoring the fact that I was pregnant and carrying on as normal; but my womb was not to be outsmarted and still I lost babies. We had the most upsetting scan ever when, at 13 weeks, we were told the baby I was carrying had a serious neural tube defect and would not survive. I had *all* the scans, there was talk of installing a live video feed from my womb direct to the early pregnancy unit. None of it made a blind bit of difference, we had tests, then some more tests, a lovely consultant told me to 'chill out'. Naturally, I told him to Fuck Off.

Every time I got pregnant again, we were on high alert and almost every time it went wrong I had no idea it had happened. I felt so stupid and embarrassed for not knowing what was going on in my own body and for letting myself have those teeny tiny moments fantasizing about life with a baby. Basically getting pregnant, for us, was a big fat mess. The folder containing my notes was like an enormous red flag alerting the health professionals to put on their most caring voices as soon as we entered the room.

I once tried to write about the 'right thing to say to someone who has just had a miscarriage' and I realised that after each one I had felt differently every single day. Sometimes I wanted the loss acknowledged, sometimes I hated the fact that people were feeling sorry for me, sometimes I wanted the support of the early pregnancy unit at the local hospital. At other times, I wanted to burn the place down.

After one miscarriage, I briefly felt sort of okay about the whole thing. There is no right way to feel after a miscarriage, so there is no right thing to say, so we don't talk about it. Certainly not around pregnant women. In essence, the gap between pregnant ladies and ladies trying to get pregnant gets wider.

There's an accepted narrative about the sadness and loss surrounding losing a baby. Miscarriage is often talked about in hushed tones, illustrated with beautiful, sad poems. But nothing I read about miscarriage really reflected how I felt about it, because the way I felt about it wasn't 'nice'.

When I saw mums pushing prams down the street I didn't well up with tears of sorrow... I wanted to punch something. Hard. For me the main overarching feeling surrounding my experience of miscarriage was anger. I was angry that what was happening was outside my control; I was furious at myself for being such a horrible person and I came to the conclusion that being such a heartless bitch was the reason my babies weren't thriving. That I was not fit to be a mother.

And now I am a mother. I can't speak for anyone else who goes through this but, for me, a few years down the line I think that miscarriage prepared me for being a mum. It taught me to roll with the punches, that babies are impossible to work out; it taught me that however much you will something to happen, sometimes life has other plans. It taught me that even when you think your world is falling apart you can still go out with friends and laugh so much it hurts.

It definitely made me more easygoing because it turns out the consultant who told me to 'chill out' was right. I didn't worry about my daughter as much because I knew she was a survivor before I even laid eyes on her. After several horrendous scan experiences my partner was shaking when we went for our 20 week scan but I was calmer because I knew this baby was strong enough; it was already kicking the crap out of my insides.

Looking back on that time I don't feel angry or even sad, I think of those lost pregnancies as part of the journey. If they had gone to plan I would be the mother of two different children (maybe even more) and I would never have got to know my son and my daughter. *That* makes me feel sad. So no, I don't remember anniversaries, missed due dates, or feel sad about the babies that didn't make it, I genuinely don't give any of that a moment's thought. Why would I? I am far too busy dealing with the day-to-day challenges of the children I *do* have, to be sad about the children I didn't have.

Challenges like *'Find the wasp spoon, Mummy!'* You know the wasp spoon? No me neither. Turns out it's the spoon my children use to scoop up dead wasps and bees, a spoon that I have been unknowingly using as, well, a spoon for quite some time now. Sorry to anyone who's ever been round mine for a cup of tea. And sorry to anyone who goes through pregnancy loss, I hope that one day you too will have the honour of owning a special spoon for picking up dead bees.

Chapter 10
Stuff we don't talk about: Money

Making the change from having a career, and your own money, to being at home looking after children is a big step, not just for you but also for your bank balance. Having a baby is a great opportunity for you to realise that material things aren't all that important but that doesn't mean that your money worries are over.

When you are tightening your belt as a couple, you will discover that things you consider to be essential purchases your partner thinks of as a waste of money. Men are often shocked at the price of a decent moisturiser when there's stuff for sale in the supermarket at a quarter of the price.

But darling I want to shop for facial skin care at a counter where the assistants wear white overalls and demonstrate serums, not have a man wearing a tabard and carrying onions point me to aisle 12. I have invested years researching these products; if you want to save money stop using my anti-aging serum on your balls after you shower.

My problem wasn't the fact that we had less money, it was the fact that I no longer had *my own* money. Not having a working wage going into your bank account is rubbish. Obviously because you have no money, but also because of feminism. It turns out that all that time I assumed I did my chosen career because I enjoyed it, I kinda did it for the money too.

Like most modern career women I was used to making and spending my money however I wanted to. I could pay my own way, I had savings to get me through the lean times and I had bought my own flat in one of the world's most expensive cities. As much as I loved *Sex And The City*, I hated the episode where Carrie realised she had spent all her money on shoes and tutus and couldn't afford to buy a flat – what a prize tit. Anyway, things have moved on since *Sex And The City*, now we're on to *Mad Men* where women are supposed to give up their jobs once they are married to concentrate on looking after babies whilst mixing cocktails and wearing fabulous dresses. Oh hang on, that's set in the swinging sixties, in modern life we get to return to work after spending our maternity leave in the library at Rhythm and Jiggle sessions where cocktails are frowned upon and fabulous dresses are impractical. Look how far we've come!

We decided on a system which involved my partner transferring money into my account for food shopping/ housekeeping on a monthly basis. I hated it. I hated seeing the money go into my bank, I hated having to spend it. I hated the fact that every now and then he forgot to transfer the money and I had to ask him for the money. It made me feel physically sick.

Buying my flat is one of the things I am most proud of, after giving birth and that time I found my way back to my tent at Glastonbury whilst drunk. After spending all those years working hard to be independent, it felt weird having to rely financially on someone else. Maybe it would have been easier if we'd been a bit more traditional in our set up instead of me deciding to start a family with a man I met whilst drunk in a field at a festival (don't worry he was incredibly good looking – I'm not an idiot). Now I was stuck at home feeling lost and useless and I loathed it.

When you are working and earning a wage you can turn a bad day at the office around with some retail therapy. 40 percent of the clothes in my wardrobe were bought for practical reasons – work, a friend's wedding, because it was stripey – the remaining 60 percent were purchased after a bad day at work. In fact, shopping would be much easier if stores laid out their clothes into two departments: 'Essentials' aka dresses for weddings and stripey tops, and 'Non Essentials' aka general lovely stuff that will make you feel better after listening to Julia in sales witter on about her dickhead boyfriend all day.

At home with a baby I still had bad days 'at the office' but the retail therapy was no longer an option. I was surprised at how much I missed having my own money. As a new mum you find yourself feeling a bit weird and unsure about everything you do and for me the lack of financial independence was just another chip, chip, chip away at the confident person I was before.

Things came to a head when my partner offered to buy me a pair of shoes. I know... how rude! I was apoplectic with rage at this kind but misguided offer. I didn't want him to buy me shoes, I wanted to buy my own shoes. I like buying my own footwear, ridiculous shiny gold boots which he thinks are 'too much' for the nursery run. They're fucking gold boots, of course they're too much... that's the entire point of them.

So if you want to avoid a meltdown in a shoe shop on a busy Saturday afternoon – and let's face it who doesn't – it's important to come up with a workable financial plan. I honestly thought that after having had a complete stranger wave their hands around in my vagina I was pretty immune to embarrassment but it turns out I was still too embarrassed to talk about our financial arrangements honestly. Which makes me just as big a tit as Carrie from *Sex and The City* but without the wardrobe full of Manolos.

Chapter 11
Choosing childcare (aka the most terrifying thing you will do EVER)

Finding and choosing a complete stranger to look after your precious first-born is a scary business. Perhaps you have two sets of adoring grandparents living close by who are able to take up the slack. Maybe you can afford your own live-in Mary Poppins. Chances are neither of these are true and, like most new parents, you are going to have to delve into the wonderful world of childcare.

Don't worry if even reading this makes you feel a bit teary. I genuinely thought that looking for someone to take care of my baby was the most terrifying thing I'd ever done. Sod the birth – at least there were drugs on offer if it all got a bit too much. But, now I was expected to make a decision about someone who would care for the fruit of my loins with no medical back up…

My first foray into childcare was not a resounding success. Living in North London and in need of some part time childcare while I started looking for work, I popped into a local nursery to check it out. I soon discovered that this was yet another aspect of parenting where I had woefully underestimated the amount of work involved. I assumed that you went, had a look around and then put your child's name on the waiting list if you liked it. What an idiot! The nursery manager gave a little snort of derision, as she explained that their waiting list was 18 months long *and* you were expected to pay a deposit to get on it.

Snorty nursery manager lady then showed me around rooms filled with babies and small children. All I could think was: *How the hell had anyone got a three-month-old baby into a nursery with an 18-month-long waiting list?* Clearly I was living amongst a breed of crazy organised mums who had happily chosen a nursery before they even got pregnant, then paid a large deposit to add one of their unfertilized eggs to a waiting list before skipping home to put a date in the diary for making babies. Yet, somehow, I was the one getting the funny looks. I was proudly shown a book of organic, locally-sourced, food suppliers and patronisingly told that spaces did sometimes come up.

Hello, it's FutureLeaders Nursery, we have a space for your child.

Oh, I'm sorry, I totally forgot to have a baby, my mistake.

Are you sure you don't have a cat you'd like to send, otherwise I'm going to have to offer the place to a someone from Yorkshire with zero forward planning skills?'

It didn't matter. I had already decided that I didn't want my baby hanging out with the offspring of crazy organised mums, and I left the little angels dribbling locally-sourced organic puree all over their chubby smug cheeks. Fuck you snorty snooty lady.

Working out how childcare works is quite a project since, aside from the practicalities, you're also negotiating a tricky emotional state. Childcare you require because you are returning to work versus childcare you require because you would quite like a break from being a parent (thank you very much) are two very different things. It's okay to walk into a childcare setting and burst into tears – they're used to it. Childcare professionals probably see just as many tears from parents as they do from the children.

When my son was a small baby I visited another nursery and left declaring that I hated it; there was not one single thing I liked about it. As soon as I stepped out of the door, I burst into tears and vowed I would never go back there. This time there was no snooty lady, no ridiculous waiting list, it was a perfectly lovely nursery but I did not really want to leave my son with anyone else so the place looked awful to me. A few months later I went back (I have a very lax attitude to vows; it's a good job I'm not married) and this time the whole nursery felt totally different, not because of any changes they had made but because I was in a completely different place myself. I was ready to leave my baby. In fact, I'd probably describe it more accurately as desperate to get rid of him for a few hours each week.

Visiting nurseries and meeting childminders is a stressful business; what questions can you possibly ask someone that will determine whether they are the right person to look after your baby? The answer is: there are none. You can write a list of things to ask but basically it all comes down to this… 'Do you feel happy leaving your children in this environment?' and mostly the answer is no. A more accurate question would be 'Do you feel, sort of, maybe, okay about leaving your child in this place with these people?' If you can answer that question with a shrug of possibility then you're halfway there.

* * * * *

Think of finding childcare as like buying property. You know immediately when something is not right for you – even though it might be absolutely lovely. Conversely, when you find the right place you'll know it immediately but then you'll still worry you're not really qualified to be making such a huge decision and will have panic attacks every time you think about it. Being a grown up is hard work!

My mum worked for many years with young children and she told me to look out for nurseries where staff got down to the children's level physically – I found a wonderful pre-school where you could always find members of staff rolling around on the floor so I think it was good advice – just check they're not drunk first.

Both my children were also looked after, part time, by two brilliant childminders; interestingly, neither of them were rated outstanding by Ofsted. When we moved to Yorkshire, I was fortunate to meet a mum at a playgroup who I didn't realise was a childminder. I just assumed she was a mum with lots of children... all with different fathers. She looked after her children, that were not actually her children, just like they were her own children, which was exactly what I wanted.

* * * * *

Here's a basic introduction to the different childcare options available.

Childminder. The calmest person in the park even though they have the most children. Usually their pockets are full of snacks and they will zip past you with a pram and four pre-school children while you struggle with a single sleeping baby. Childminders often care for children in their own homes so their front rooms are full of plastic shit. However many times you have seen *Frozen*, they have seen it more.

Day Nursery. Offering flexible childcare for children from three months until they start school. Not full time mind, you have to pick them up at the end of the day. Do not piss off staff at your child's nursery or they will encourage your child to make a giant cityscape out of empty boxes and milk bottles which they will send you home with on a windy day.

Pre-school. From two years onwards. A place where children learn through play and prepare themselves for going to school by returning home in someone else's knickers every day. Pre-schools operate during term time only and often don't have the most flexible of sessions. If you think the staff at pre-school are looking at you funny it's because your child has told them all about the argument Mummy and Daddy had last night. Including the bit where you made up.

Nanny. A mythical creature who moves in and looks after your children, teaching them to tidy up whilst singing songs. May have wings or a tail. I have never actually met a real life nanny although I did once mistake someone's housekeeper for a nanny – how embarrassing!

Au Pair. Young person who looks after your children in exchange for board, meals and pocket money. Contrary to popular belief they are unlikely to actually sleep with either you or your partner – have you looked in the mirror recently?

Once you've found the right place you will have to go through the challenging 'settling in' period. A settling in period is basically two/three weeks of extreme emotional trauma where both you and your child can expect to burst into tears at any given moment. The major difference is that one of you will be given cuddles, a biscuit and encouraged to paint a crappy picture of a dog while the other one is left sobbing in the car outside the supermarket looking like a weirdo.

I went through two opposing ends of the nursery settling in experience. My daughter just walked in from day one and told me to go away while all the other mums got to fuss and feel wanted. I mean I'm not a total bitch but it would have been nice if she could have at least been a little bit upset about not spending time with Mummy.

Be careful what you wish for.

When it was my son's turn, he screamed and begged me not to leave him, every day for a whole month, leaving scratch marks on my arms and legs where he refused to let go. Hearing your child sob, '*No Mummy No! Please don't leave me here!*' is not the best start to the day. So, if you are going back to work it's worth taking the horrendous crying into account as you probably don't want to be heading into the office, for your first day back, after dealing with this. Sod's law is that they will settle in fine and start kicking off when you go to work anyway. Often small children will spend their first few days or weeks happily enjoying nursery before they realise what's going on; then they will start the daily morning sobfest.

The first day your child is at nursery is tough for mum. Here's a list of suggested things to do with your day to make sure you make the most of it.

1. Try not to burst into tears at the nursery – retain some dignity by hiding in the bushes outside and blubbing instead. Wonder why the bush is stuffed full of empty cardboard boxes covered in glitter and paint.

2. Go home and have a nice cup of tea.

3. Make another cup of tea because your first was a bit cold and salty from all the tears.

4. Think about calling the nursery 'just to check in'. DO NOT ACTUALLY CALL THE NURSERY they will hate you for it and your child's shit pictures will never make it to the wall[6]

5. Write a list of all the jobs you need to get done.

6. Cross out any jobs that involve housework, going to the supermarket, or not sitting on the sofa eating cake.

7. Sit on sofa and eat cake.

---

[6] Not true, they will literally put any old crap on the walls.

8. Fill in all the 'About your child' forms that the nursery has given you to avoid your son being sent home three months later with a painting of a family tree that says Mummy? Daddy? Brothers? Sisters? Pets? instead of actual names. Yes, this did actually happen to us.

9. Go to collect child from nursery, spot other parents shoving crappy glittery box artwork in the bushes. That's one mystery solved.

If your child is at nursery, and is old enough to talk – do not expect them to tell you anything about their day. For example, what they have been doing or who they've played with. This is entirely normal. There is a code of silence at pre-school and nursery like the Mafia code of Omerta but more strictly adhered to. What happens at pre-school stays at pre-school. Unless it causes a physical injury and then you get a form to sign and an explanation.

It's tempting to leave a huge long list of instructions for anyone who is looking after your child, detailing all your child's favourite songs and the correct key to sing them in. If you do feel the urge to annotate your copy of *The Gruffalo* with stage directions to ensure the animals all have the 'right' voices, that's fine – but don't actually do it.

When they are with their parents your child may demand that you sing *'ricey cakes, ricey cakes, nom, nom, nicey cakes'* every time you give her a snack, but she will happily chomp through packets of rice cakes when Grandma is looking after her, silently. Children are annoying like that, they save all their worst bits for the people they're closest to. Just like we do as adults.

My son started walking at nine months old – his twig-like little legs propelled him at great speed across parks, into walls and along streets, but by the time he turned two he could not be bothered to walk. It was as though he realised he'd started too early and now he was having a rest. He couldn't even make it from the car into the house, throwing his arms up and screaming *Carry! Carry!* any time his feet were expected to make contact with the floor. We live on the edge of the moors in Yorkshire but we couldn't get anywhere near them without a complete meltdown. Unless he was with the childminder, that is. Somehow she managed to get three whole two year olds (plus a dog) up a great big hill nearly every day. I have no idea how she managed it.

The one thing you can be sure of is that your child will behave completely differently when they are not with Mummy and Daddy. Try to concentrate on this more positive aspect of childcare when you are panicking about returning to work. And know that all that time explaining how little Bobby hates carrots and *has* to have his food off a green plate is a total waste of time. Your children will do things you never dreamed possible whilst under someone else's care, like eating carrots off a red plate or even using their legs.

Chapter 12
What does a mum look like?

What do *you* think a mum looks like? Go on ask yourself the question. I don't know exactly how I would have answered that question before I had babies, but I know that however I described her she would have been different to myself, a bit more… sensible, mature. Wearing a boring coat. That's it! Boring.

I have literally no idea where I got this idea from, my own mum is not boring and her mum was the least boring woman I have ever met; none of my friends who have children are boring or became even a tiny bit boring when they had kids. I could write a list a mile long of mums I know who are great mums but in no way sensible or mature. In fact, I could write a pretty long list of mums who you would do well to avoid if you want to retain your sanity and some sense of dignity (but hey who wants to do that?!).

So why the hell does it still make me shift uncomfortably in my seat when I am labelled as a mum? This is clearly ridiculous… I've got two children, and the number of times I hear the word *Mummy!* during the day is off the chart. Thinking that mums were somehow different to me – that they felt differently or behaved differently to myself made me feel as though I was on the outside looking in at motherhood. A lot of the time, it has felt like I was playing at being a proper mum.

I suppose a little bit of this was me being a tosser. I thought I was cooler than everyone else; I thought I was different. I'd moved away from home, forged a career, I didn't necessarily want the same things as 'everyone else'. Until I did. As soon as my sister had children my ovaries went into overdrive and I wanted a baby; it was not a decision made over late night discussions with a long term partner... it was as though something hormonal had exploded inside me and I needed to get going right away. So I did.

When I realised I wanted children it almost felt like a bit of a betrayal – having a family is such a normcore thing to do. I think I thought having a family, moving back home, and giving up work to look after children was a cop out. A few years down the line I am at peace with my normality because now I understand that it is completely possible to be a mum and still be the same person you were before. You don't stop finding dumb things funny when you have a baby although, in the very early days, laughing too much can cause leakage problems. If anything I find life even more hilarious now I'm a mum, I'm probably even less mature and sensible than I was before. I don't ever remember doing an entire supermarket shop whilst pretending to be a crab before I had children.

Let me make this very clear – some aspects of being a stay at home mum are dull as shit – but lots of the day is actually a proper good laugh. It's okay to find aspects of childcare tedious, it's okay to still want to do other things with your life, you can still ace it as a stay at home mum and never make a cupcake or a homemade thank you card. Mums are not boring, some of the stuff we are expected to do is tedious but it turns out you can totally stay at home and look after children and still really, really enjoy yourself, although occasionally you will have to carry a screaming toddler into the garden and leave him there while you read *Stylist* because he is getting right on your tits.

So it's worth taking the time to consider what you think a mum is, and remembering that there are lots of different ways to be a mum, and many of those ways do not involve buying a boring coat.

There are also physical changes that come with being a mum. Since writing about parenting I've had several requests to write about what happens to your lady bits after having a baby. Apparently there are people out there that want to know if their vagina will look different after they've had a baby. Do you? Maybe I'm swimming against the tide here but it never crossed my mind what my vagina would look like after I'd had a baby. Who the hell knows what their own vagina looks like? I couldn't pick mine out of a police lineup. Before or after. Maybe I'm wrong and everyone reading this book could describe their foof perfectly to police in the event of an emergency but I'm happy to be out on a limb on this one.

There's no escaping the fact that your vagina is going to have a tough time of it. Mine definitely behaves differently after having babies but then it's all old and tired now. However you give birth, pregnancy itself has a detrimental effect on your pelvic floor. Pelvic floor muscles are one of those things you only really think about once it's too late. I slightly regret the fact that I never really enjoyed spending quality time with my fully functioning pelvic floor muscles before it was too late. I should have been nicer to them, more appreciative.

The first time I took any notice of them was when I was pregnant and they were already on the way to ruin. It was like discovering I had a beautiful chocolate cake in the cupboard I didn't know about, and then immediately dropping it on the floor. Into shit. Anyway, your vagina will probably look different but who cares because unless fashions change radically *no one is going to see it*. As women, we have enough to worry about without having to concern ourselves about the bits no one sees.

Why not worry about the rest of your body instead? Although your body is no longer just your body; once you've had a baby it becomes 'your post-baby body' which makes me want to throw up just writing it. The main problem I have with the words 'post-baby body' is that it's absolute bullshit. You're not post-baby at all – you are very much *with* baby, a baby that goes everywhere you go. All that 'free time' when you are 'off work' that you thought you could use to get back into shape evaporates as it turns out you haven't got the time, the energy, or the inclination to go to the gym.

Most of what is written about the post-baby body concentrates on the way it looks because, guess what, it turns out if you grow an entire other human being inside you, your body starts to look a little different. Your body is going to change. For a while. And then it will gradually start looking a bit like the body you knew before (although you will not be able to remember exactly if that lumpy bit was always there or if you can blame it on the baby which means it doesn't count).

The good news is that you have less time to inspect it as you will be busy running around after a baby. The bad news is: biscuits. As your babies get older you will realise that 80 percent of parenting is biscuits, and that there are very few parenting problems which cannot be solved with a liberal application of biscuits.

I started running again after my second baby mainly because it gave me time out of the house alone. Often, I just ran around the corner to a nice bench and sat there in silence thinking about all the nappies and bedtime fights I was missing out on. Running doesn't sound so bad when you look at it like that does it? After having babies, running was hard work; for a start there were boobs to contend with, massive leaky sore things that actually wobbled. Added to this was the need to go for a wee every ten minutes. Even when I managed to put in some effort it felt like my body was conspiring against me. I noticed when I got back into my stride and had a good run I felt absolutely exhausted the next day. Turns out exercising can be quite tiring.

The obvious solution is to try something a little more gentle, like an exercise DVD you can do at home while your baby sleeps. What a brilliant plan! Baby can enjoy some vital tummy time whilst you perfect your downward facing dog. There is literally nothing I can think of that would stop this from happening. Why isn't every new mum doing exercise DVD's every day? Come on lazy bones get up off the sofa and... oh yeah just change that nappy first, and then a feed, and *then* you can get started (once you've jiggled the baby to sleep).

In the real world, exercise DVD's are just as tricky as getting to the gym. Davina and I spent many, many happy hours in my front room exercising. (Hi Jackie!) So many hours. The DVD was only 30 minutes long but it took all bloody day to get through it once you factor in all the feeding and nappy changing stops. Oh and hiding on the floor in embarrassment every time anyone walked past the window.

The trick is not to panic too much about losing the weight; try to ignore the fact that your fantasy celebrity BFF is already rocking up to premieres in a skin tight dress. Not sure who your fantasy celebrity BFF is? Everyone has one. Think about it... someone in the public eye who has a baby about the same time as you. You will have had absolutely no interest in this person until you discover you are going to become mums together, then you will start following their pregnancy with great interest, daydreaming about how you will hang out together on play dates, comparing sore nipples, and chatting about what a bellend her hubby Kanye is.

Chances are your fantasy celebrity BFF will start Instagramming pictures of herself doing a yoga headstand in a pair of tiny pants several short weeks after giving birth. How could she do this to you? What a bitch! And you were so close! I mean, not *actually* close – you've never even met – but you would definitely have hit it off apart from all the yoga nonsense.

Remember, just like Instagram is not your friend, neither are celebrities you've never met who appear in the sidebar of the *Daily Mail* website. Anyway who'd be famous? Life is hard enough as a new mum without having to deal with photographers snapping pictures of you pushing your pram through town and reading headlines commenting on the state of your arse. No thanks! The only time I ever want to see myself featured in the national press is if I'm hiding behind one of those massive lottery checks, cackling whilst spraying champagne all over my grinning face and talking shit about how I'm not going to let it change me.

I'd love to tell you that there's no point judging yourself against other mums you see in the papers or in the Doctor's surgery. That you should be proud of having a body that has nurtured and expelled another human being. That you shouldn't waste those precious first few months with your new baby worrying about being a bit wibbly wobbly. I'd love to tell you this because it's absolutely the truth. But it's also total bullshit.

It's a lovely idea for us all to embrace our bodies and be proud of the stretch marks and lumpy bits but, if I'm going to be honest, I really just wanted everything to get 'back to normal' after I'd had my babies, especially after having baby number two. I clearly remember wishing away those precious first few months with my adorable baby son and dreaming of the day when I could fit back into my skinny jeans. I do slightly wish I'd not been so bothered about it, but when you're in the middle of the baby whirlwind it's sometimes hard to see the bigger picture.

Remember this when you are trapped on the sofa under a sleeping baby and don't waste your time listing all the things you could be doing – cleaning, exercising, filling in that baby book you were given by someone who clearly doesn't have children. Instead, just enjoy being a nice soft resting place for your baby. Stick the skinny jeans in the loft and make the most of those precious moments because you've actually already enrolled yourself in nature's boot camp. In no time at all you'll be squatting, lifting and running after a toddler. Then you will *really* look like a mum. Nothing says 'mum' more than squawking 'Put that down now!' whilst wrestling a dirty flip flop out of a two-year-old's mouth.

Chapter 13
Beyond the first few months

Once you have a baby you will be bombarded with handy guides featuring the developmental milestones your child should be hitting and when. Just in case you didn't have enough stuff to worry about, now you can start panicking that your child is falling behind because at three months old she prefers headbutting the floor in anger instead of gurgling and laughing during tummy time.

As a parent, you are constantly in a state of waiting and willing the next developmental stage to happen, then discovering, too late, that your time would have been better spent enjoying the stage your baby was at *before* they developed this new skill which has actually just made things even harder.

It will be easier when they sleep through the night/ start weaning/ have all their teeth! you chirp.

She won't be so frustrated when she can sit up/ crawl/ walk/ buy her own drinks at the bar. they tell you. Bollocks!

The beauty of babies is that with every step forward comes an equal and opposite step backwards. They sit up – they fall over, they eat – they poo, they talk – they don't stop, they sleep through the night – oh hang on there's no downside when that happens.

But don't start celebrating just yet. Be wary of the sleep delusion, the notion that babies sleeping through the night is some kind of stage your child will reach and once you've hit that point the sleepless nights are behind you.

Many babies do start to sleep through the night and that's brilliant, for them and their mothers, and who knows maybe you will be that one mum swooshing into playgroup all refreshed and wearing laundered clothes with hair that's been washed in actual shampoo and not that stuff from a can. I'm happy for you. No, I'm sure the rest of the mums are too, it just looks like they're giving you daggers because they're all so frickin' tired. Do tell us all once again how having too much sleep can make you feel tired.

Babies do not start sleeping through the night and that's it, problem solved, because that would be too simple. Babies may start sleeping through the night but then they may also start waking up every three to four hours for a laugh. Except they're not laughing… they're screaming. The basic rule of thumb is this: as soon as you have got used to the way things are with a baby – they change. 'This too shall pass' – the good bits and the bad.

After the initial shock of bringing baby home, you hit the honeymoon period when you discover that babies actually like the noise of a bustling bar. Make the most of those long, lazy Sunday afternoons in the pub chatting with your friends as your baby sleeps in their pram.

We can still do this! Nothing has to change! First time parents cheer. And then it happens.

One day you will leave your baby for a miniscule amount of time, for example – the time it takes to jiggle a tea bag in a cup of peppermint tea, and by the time you turn back around your baby will be somewhere else. If you left them on the sofa they may have 'moved' to the floor, sometimes they can be in a completely different room or on top of a table.

No one know how they do this – a baby's first movements are almost never seen by the human eye. The first time it happens you don't even know it's happened, thinking instead that this is sleep deprivation playing tricks on you. Obviously you forgot where you had put the baby, silly Mummy! When you do eventually see your baby moving for the first time, your heart swells with pride and elation. Immediately, you call your nearest and dearest, and if they are parents themselves they will all be thinking the same thing: You can kiss those lazy Sunday lunches in the pub goodbye.

There is an enormous difference between having a baby that can be contained in a pram or car seat and having a baby that moves about. Before your baby starts moving, life had all been about managing a child that cries, poos, wees, and feeds in a static position. Now you are dealing with the same problems but *not all in the same place*. This is a momentous change – expect to spend all your time from this point onwards stopping your child from trying to injure itself, they usually start with eating rubbish off the floor, falling down stairs or getting stuck under the sofa before moving onto stepping out into traffic and falling down flights of stone stairs into rivers.

To make matters even more interesting, babies start moving about the same time as weaning commences creating the perfect shitstorm. Literally. Better be on good terms with your vacuum cleaner – you are going to be spending a lot of time together.

Soon after your baby starts moving you will experience 'that time at the pub/ cafe/ park'... aka the day when everything goes wrong. One day out that will scar you so deeply it will change the course of future events. There's a poo incident, followed by a sick incident, all drowned out by some screaming and then a massive shouty argument over who forgot to pack the spare sleepsuit. Your pub lunch goes untouched as you abandon your friends to rush home, sweaty and stressed with a poo-stained cardigan and an angry red-faced baby wearing a sleepsuit fashioned out of Daddy's shirt and an elastic hairband. The cheer of "We can still do this!" is drowned out by the sobs of "We are never leaving the house again!'

For the next few months, while your baby wakes up and starts exploring the world, you stay in *a lot*. This is partly because you don't want to inflict the full horror of having a baby that moves on the rest of the world but also because you are too embarrassed to go back to the scene of the crime.

Instead, you start throwing dinner parties at home because that's what people with babies do. There are only two reasons people throw dinner parties: either they have spent all their money on buying a property, which they want to show off, or they are too scared to go out in public with small children.

Don't worry, it's not forever. In a few years, you will be able to return to the pub armed with a smartphone full of pirate dress up apps and animal noise quizzes. You will once again hang out with your friends while your sulky toddler accidentally snapchats your boss and spends a fortune downloading virtual pirate treasure. Ahoy there matey! Level 2 complete!

Developmental timeline for Mothers from 0 - 18 months. Here is a useful list of developmental milestones you will hit as a mother. Don't worry if you don't hit them all at the 'right time', this is just a guide, remember every mother is different and will develop at a different pace.

0 - 6 weeks: Blind panic, no sleep, sore tits.

6 - 12 weeks: Less panicking at home and more panicking in cafes, shops and on public transport. Lots of talking about your vagina. Looking at other mums and wondering how they're all doing it better than you.

3 - 6 months: Start going to groups and making friends with everybody. Googling 'teething' every 20 minutes. Using lack of sleep as an excuse for general slovenliness. Start getting excited about weaning when really you should be throwing a farewell party for all the nice stuff in your house.

6 - 12 months: Feeling bad cos your baby fell off the sofa. Feeling bad because your kitchen is fucked now you've started weaning. Feeling bad for avoiding that one mum you made friends with at playgroup who turned out to be nuts. Using teething as an excuse for all the mess. Tutting at parents of older kids who knock your baby over at soft play.

12 - 18 months: Backache from having to hold a toddler's hand at an awkward angle while they learn to walk properly. Pretending their first word wasn't 'backpack' which they learned from *Dora the Explorer*. Repeatedly answering the same two questions: Are you having another one? When are you going back to work? I DON'T KNOW!

18 months - 3 years: Still looking at other mums and thinking how much better they are doing than you but caring less about it. Excited about saying goodbye to nappies. Crying over all the nice stuff you used to have that's now ruined.

3 - 4 years: Shouting a lot. Googling the answer to a million different crazy questions every day including 'How did mums answer toddlers' questions before the Internet?' Freaking out over school applications. Being tutted at in soft play when your child knocks over a baby. Looking at other mums and realising everyone is doing as badly as you.

Extended maternity leave: I am not a stay at home mum! After a year at home with a baby, the fun really starts. By fun, I mean tantrums, frustration and public humiliation. Toddlers are literally the best fun you can have and (as we all know) having the best time of your life always comes with some kind of fallout. For every amazing night out there's an equally spectacular hangover, the parties where you have the best fun always leave you with a ruined dress and a missing shoe or a work colleague you can never look in the eye again. Owning a toddler is an invite to the craziest party in town… every day. You just have to learn to embrace the public embarrassment and enjoy the madness.

The problem is that just as your baby starts to get interesting, it's often time to go back to work. And that's when you realise you might actually want to stay at home a little longer; even though you love work, you love being a mum more.

Obviously I was going back to work, right? I wasn't chucking away all that hard work climbing the career ladder just to give up once I'd had a baby. That's what I thought, hell, that's what I said, ignoring everyone else mumbling about how I'd see things differently once the baby arrived.

When I was pregnant, I genuinely believed I would be back at work by the time my baby was three months old. But, after a year, I was still enjoying being at home with my daughter and I realised I *wanted* to stay at home, even if that did make me officially, whisper it, a stay at home mother.

If I had trouble identifying myself as a mum, well, you can imagine the challenge I had at being labelled a stay at home mum with all the cupcake baking and craft sessions I stupidly assumed it entailed. Even worse, on internet forums Stay At Home Mum is abbreviated to SAHM which makes it sound like an evil force from The *Lord of the Rings* trilogy.

Behold SAHM! Servant of Sauron, sister of Saruman, commander of the Uruk-Hai and mum to an unruly toddler. Fancy coming round for a playdate?

Once you are on extended maternity leave, life changes a little – your support network of amazing mum friends starts to shrink and the baby buddies that got you through those early months will – one by one – return to work or move halfway across the country to be nearer family (how dare they!) leaving you with fewer people to hang out with during the day. Eventually, it's just you... the boring mumsy types left.

Oh, hang on! Wait a minute, that's me and all my friends I'm talking about! We're not boring mumsy types!

Just as I had been surprised earlier by what makes a mum, now I found myself re-evaluating my prejudices about stay at home mums. The good news is they weren't boring housewives on a mission to make the perfect cupcake. The bad news is it turns out that I can be incredibly judgemental about other women I have never even met. What a bitch!

Choosing to stay at home with your children does not make you boring, although being at home looking after children can be a teeny bit dull. Many of the mums I met were women who had climbed so far up the career ladder it was impractical for them to return to work in their previous job and fit in a fun family life. More on this appalling state of affairs later.

For the first few months that I was busy learning how to look after a baby, I was tired and stressed and too busy to be bored or lonely. But, after a year, I was hitting my stride being a mum. I could get out and about with no real issues. But even with a fairly large network of mum friends and non-mum friends to meet up with, loneliness was starting to bite. My children mean everything to me, they are the most wonderful things I have ever done and I adore every last molecule of their beings, but God help me spending day after day alone with a toddler and a baby made me want to cry with boredom. So I did.

The most frustrating thing was the daily battle to leave the house. Before children, I was amazing at getting out of the house; if I had been a superhero that would have been my special power.

Is it a bird? Is it a plane? No, it's 'Arriving At Places On Time And In Clean Clothes Girl!'

Okay, so the name needs a bit of work, but you get the idea.

But that all changed when I had children to deal with. I was constantly running late. I know it's wrong to blame the children for everything but I've thought long and hard about this and it was definitely their fault. Small children were the Kryptonite to my punctuality-based superpowers.

I read an interview with Sarah Jessica Parker where she compared leaving the house with small children to a military operation. Now I have never been invited on a military operation – unlike SJP (what on earth did she wear?) – but I doubt very much they involve everyone sitting on the hall floor crying, and wearing one shoe each, twenty minutes after you're already meant to be somewhere. If military operations *are* like this, I have seriously missed my calling.

The front door is the wooden-panelled backdrop to all my biggest failings. Every time I look at it I see all the moaning and crying and shouting, and refusing to go out without seventeen jigsaws, and a drawer full of plastic spoons; even though we are only actually driving two minutes down the road to nursery because we are already too late to walk there. Just put your coat on, PLEASE. Yes back to front, I don't care.

The worst bit was expending so much time and energy trying to get everyone out of the house to go places I *didn't even really want to go to*. Much as I think playgroups and parks are wonderful places to keep children entertained, they are not my choice of day out. I wouldn't mind the children kicking up such a stink if we were off to the Alexander McQueen exhibition at the Victoria and Albert Museum but, no, I found myself exhausted after fighting over lost shoes and missing coats just so I could spend the morning at soft play drinking crap coffee and plucking up the courage to make small talk with another bored (not boring) mum.

The reason you find yourself dragging children out of the house is because while staying at home may seem like the easy option at ten in the morning, it turns into a big mistake come three o'clock in the afternoon when you have been home alone all day and have forgotten how to speak in full sentences.

Sometimes the days seemed to stretch out forever. I started to feel disconnected with the world around me, it was as though everyone else was getting on, and doing stuff, while I was sat at home being incredibly dull. This was brought sharply into focus when I finished binge-watching *The West Wing*. I was traumatised when I watched the last episode. Watching CJ, Donna and Josh making the fictional world a better place was all I had in life and once they were gone I felt empty and alone. I spent at least a week crying about that show ending. Then I discovered *Mad Men* and life perked up again.

But before you call your boss and start ironing smart trousers, there are of course positives to staying at home with a small child for longer than a year. The days of panicking every time you leave the house are over and now conversation starts to widen; you find yourself talking less about bodily functions and how much sleep you've had, and more about books you've read, current affairs or whether it's normal to have a crush on the dragon with the sexy voice from *Mike The Knight* (apparently it's not).

Extended maternity leave can be great fun, it's when you get to spend quality time with your babies watching them do stuff. Finally, those picnics in the park that your partner fantasized about all those months before are now reality. And so, you start thinking about other ways you could throw your life into complete disarray. Like having another baby or going back to work.

Babies and Careers. Eventually a return to work is inevitable, maybe after your first baby, maybe after your second, perhaps after your fifth – who knows where this crazy parenting ride will take you…

The thing to remember is this: returning to work after having a baby is going to be hard work, because y'know work is sort of hard work, but it is also nothing you cannot handle. How long a career break you take is usually a decision driven by many different factors but the main one is money. Lots of mums find themselves returning to work after about a year, and gap of up to twelve months in your CV can always be painted in a positive light.

'Yeah I took a year out, climbed Machu Picchu/ built a school/ became a yoga instructor/ had a baby.'

All these things seem like they're *adding* to your skillset in some way, even if nine of the twelve months were actually spent watching *Bargain Hunt* in your pyjamas. But whether you've been at home for six months or six years, all parents returning to work face the same important challenges: Can I still do this? and What the hell am I going to wear? The answers are: Yes, Clothes.

All my friends who have returned to the same job have reported the same thing: after just one week it feels like you've never been away. Which is great to hear but doesn't help with the first day back. There's no getting over the fact that your first day will be tough and it is normal to feel nervous, out of the loop, and to miss your baby. The best thing you can do is to rally the troops and have friends and family text you supportive messages throughout the day. You've done this before and there's no reason why you can't do this again. Remind yourself of that, when you are locked in a toilet cubicle having a bit of a cry at lunchtime. At least you'll be in there on your own.

When I had my first baby, I didn't return to work because having worked freelance I had no work to return to. Lots of my friends did have jobs to go back to, though, and many of them chose not to do so, largely because they enquired about the possibility of perhaps working part time (or more flexible hours so they could be a mum as well) and they were all told no thank you. It was infuriating to watch all these talented, hard-working women being pushed out of the workplace and discovering exactly how inflexible the world of work really is.

The good news is that, as a stay at home mum, I acquired a selection of extremely competent and well-qualified ladies to sing *The Wheels on The Bus* with, at Clappy Times Nursery Rhymes sessions. I couldn't help thinking that this was not the way things should be. Obviously, this needs to change; a world that these women loved, and had been proud to be part of, now wanted nothing to do with them. When faced with what seemed an impossible task, these women did what comes naturally to them: they moaned and stamped their feet petulantly. Then they remembered that while moaning and stamping your feet might get a toddler a biscuit, it's rarely a winning strategy in the world of work. So I watched as career-women-turned-mums dusted off their CV's and paraded up and down in front of the mirror trying to decide how far out of fashion their smart clothes were.

If you had a career once... you can have a career again. It is entirely possible to be successful at work and at home. However, like most things in life it's hard. But the good news is that having a career break can be a catalyst for change. Lots of my friends have used extended maternity leave to reconsider their careers, to fight for part time work at the same level, to set up their own businesses or to just do something completely different. It's been amazing seeing how starting a family has galvanised successful women into action. No mum wants to be away from their children all the time but if you are going to spend time at work you realise it's important to make your time at work count, whether the rewards are financial or personal, or even both if you get lucky.

But if you want to go back to work, you have to find it first. Finding work after a career break presents a big challenge – for starters there are interviews to contend with. Job interviews are naturally stressful and when you're not feeling on top of your game they can become terrifying.

If contestants on *The Apprentice* are the ultimate in pompous boasting, women returning to work after a career break are the Yin to their Yang. While the super-confident sharp-suited business types brag about their scant achievements, mothers returning to work wipe baby sick off the only smart-ish skirt they own and mumble about not having done anything much in the past year. A year in which they have faced more challenges than they ever did at the office.

The problem is that managing the expectations of an inflexible person with a demanding schedule is only good for your CV if that person is out of nappies. Looking after a baby doesn't translate to skills on your CV. To the world of work, you've been doing the same thing day after day and, after more than a year doing the same thing, that gap in your résumé starts to open up like a chasm. You're no longer adding skills to your CV you're losing them – getting rusty, out of touch, left behind.

I spoke to a mother and former lawyer the other day who explained that she was 'de-skilled' as she jiggled her baby in a sling with one hand and refixed a four-year-old's ponytail with the other, managing to keep them both from bursting into tears on the walk to school.

In reality, looking after a baby is not 'doing the same thing' day after day. As babies grow, and develop new skills, so do their parents. Every new developmental stage brings new challenges; there are things you can do with baby wipes when you have a 15-month-old you wouldn't have dreamed possible when you were a new mum. But I'm still not sure where to put advanced baby wipe skills on my CV - Personal Interests? Vocational Training? Skills and Abilities? It's very confusing.

What about my ability to carry out a range of everyday tasks single-handedly? And by that I don't mean on my own, I mean on my own *with just one hand*. Really what any mum in a job interview wants to say is this:

You know all that shit you used to throw at me? Well now I have wipes. Bring it on.

My first interview after having a baby – in front of a panel of four men for a senior role I had literally NO prior experience in – was understandably dreadful. After three years explaining things simply and slowly to small children I got carried away with the excitement of adult conversation and babbled away like a crazy person. It makes me cringe a little to think about it now, but it wasn't a complete waste of time. Obviously sitting in front of people explaining that you have no idea what the job they are interviewing for entails is not ideal, so I chose to concentrate on the fact that I got an interview. Somehow, somewhere in that process, people looked at my CV and thought I might be worth seeing. Thinking about it, that interview was brilliant for me. If you're going to make a tit of yourself, it might as well be for a job you were unlikely to get in the first place.

Finding work that fits around being a mum is difficult but finding a great job has always been challenging. That's the whole point of having a good career, it's hard work getting to where you want to be, but not impossible. I've watched my friends set up their own businesses, find consultancy work and fight for the right to work from home. Mothers who return to work after having a baby aren't de-skilled… they are determined and hardworking and ready for the challenge. Companies that let women go because they refuse to consider any changes to the way they worked previously are making a big mistake. But that's the way things are. So, it's up to us to change that.

There's no doubt that having a baby messes with the flow of your career but it can also be a brilliant opportunity. Many of my friends who had babies towards the end of their thirties were already getting a little bit fed up with their jobs and hitting the reset button on their careers, with a break to start a family, gave them the breathing space to work out what they really wanted to do with the rest of their lives.

When my sister and I were young, both my parents jacked in their jobs to start afresh. My mum who had missed out on the opportunity to go to university when she was younger decided to go back and study to be a teacher, and my dad set up his own business as an antique dealer. If you were to ask me about my parents, I would tell you Mum was a teacher and Dad was/is an antique dealer (there's no retiring from antiques) but they only took on these roles in their forties.

Starting a family doesn't have to be the end of a career. It could also be the start of a new one. If your old workplace 'doesn't do part time', then why not team up with a colleague in a similar position and apply for roles as a job share? Setting up your own business is definitely not an easy option but working on your own project in-between trying to toddler wrangle is how many successful enterprises have been born. Sitting at home watching *Paw Patrol* on repeat is the perfect opportunity to start thinking about work and hatching plans.

So what do you want to do with the rest of your life?

Chapter 14
Relocation
Relocation
Relocation

Once you have a baby, and that baby starts moving about and causing trouble, you start to look at the space you live in completely differently, through the eyes of a worried parent. You realise that everything you own is basically a death trap and all your artsy fartsy knick knacks with pointy bits sticking out of them start to make their way slowly up the shelves until they end up migrating into a box in the garage. You can spot the house of parents with a newly-moving baby because everything below knee height has been removed. It's the only time I've ever really cleaned a skirting board.

As well as realising you live in a death trap, your home also starts to shrink; entire rooms are taken over with jumperoos, changing mats and boxes of noisy plastic crap. All your prized possessions get bumped down the list of preference too. The antique ceremonial mask you bought in Bali that no one was allowed to touch, ever, now becomes an integral part of your peek-a-boo games to distract a teething baby.

Your home also appears to have repositioned itself to the worst part of town. Where once you loved being next door to that cool Brazilian bar with the late night samba dancing lock-ins, now you just notice the vomit-stained streets and how the bottle bin clanks every single time your baby has just fallen asleep. Where once you were vicariously entertained by overhearing the bar staff discussing their convoluted love lives now you just want to have a nap at 2pm in the afternoon. Once you've found yourself shouting 'Just chuck him – he's a knob!' out of the bathroom window you realise it's time for a rethink.

And so you and your partner start to re-evaluate your lives and that's when one of you chirps, *'I know what would make our lives better, let's move to the other end of the country!'* Because obviously that would help, right?

Okay, so not everyone has such a drastic thought but there are a lot of parents who start to realise that they might quite like to live near grandparents so that their children can get to know them better, and Mummy and Daddy can go out to the cinema every now and again. If you do decide to relocate, here are a few things you might want to consider.

Firstly we did it, we moved from London to Yorkshire when our children were two years and six months old. We did it because we had a family support network waiting for us in Yorkshire, we had friends, and if I'm honest I was hoping my children would acquire a nice broad Yorkshire accent (this hasn't happened yet).

We moved from North London and a 20-minute tube ride to everything the capital has to offer to a lovely town in Yorkshire that is famous for having two massive rocks and a song about a decomposing corpse. I am not even making that up. To be fair the song does have a very catchy tune.

But while big rocks and sheep are nice to look at, they aren't going to meet you in Starbucks to dissect last night's episode of *The Good Wife…* here's a few things to consider if you're thinking of making the move to a new area.

1. There is never a right time to relocate. Choosing the 'right time' to relocate is like deciding when to have a baby.

There is no one time that will be easier than the rest; whenever you do it, it will be a long painful process, but hopefully one that makes things better for you in the long run. Just pick whatever suits you best and go for it, remember it's only a massive life-changing decision you're making. How bad can it be!?!

2. You will have to start all over again with the baby friends thing. Urgh I know! Take a long hard look at yourself in the mirror, and tell yourself you can do this! Starting all over again looking for baby friends is hard work. It was hard work the first time around but learning a whole set of new names and stories is exhausting. Also, there is something magical about the new mum camaraderie that engulfs you when you are all discovering how to manage a baby together. Once your babies are a few months old you've been through so much with your mum friends you feel relaxed with them. It seems completely normal to chat about your lady garden with them. For me, dropping into a group when our babies were older meant that bond wasn't there, so it took longer to get to the point where we chatted about our vaginas. Actually, now I'm writing this down, it doesn't really seem like a negative point at all.

I think I was also less confident at approaching new people. I was so desperate to make friends when I was a new mum that I threw myself into it without really thinking about it. Everything about that time is frickin' crazy so I let myself get swept away with it all and was more than happy to plonk myself down and start chatting to complete strangers. With a toddler and a six-month-old in tow, making friends was more challenging.

Where once your baby was a shortcut to making friends, having a toddler is like applying friend repellent. Toddlers don't really play with one another and woe betide anyone who dares to strike up a conversation with Mummy. Making new friends is embarrassing enough without your two-year-old shouting 'I don't like that new girl' at every potential playdate in the park.

Even the most basic of conversations are stressful when your child insists on hanging round your neck demanding you play with them immediately and stop chatting to 'these boring ladies'.

3. You can't do it all online. You can research a place online and find out everything about schools and parks and house prices but nothing really beats going there and spending a day in the park, watching all the other mums and thinking, 'Would I hate these people?' Visiting a place for however short a time will give you more of a feel than reading a thread on an Internet chat forum.

With our Yorkshire move, we didn't end up settling in the first place we chose, for many different reasons, but mainly because we went for a day out to the park somewhere else where I saw lots of mums wearing clothes I liked. Obviously don't tell the boys this, men seem to think that making life-changing decisions based on seeing a stranger wearing a mid-season jacket from Whistles is a little bit flaky. But it worked for us.

4. It takes a year longer than you think it will to settle. It takes a long time to really settle somewhere new. Three years in and we have our own front door, our youngest child can do a brilliant impersonation of Jon Snooow from *Game of Thrones* and there are no regrets.

However, it has taken all of those three years for us to really feel settled. I can chart my progress as a mum via the holidays. School holidays, as you will discover, are a nightmare for parents of small children, even though they don't directly affect you when you have a baby. For starters, all those volunteers running playgroups decide to take their good will and bugger off on holiday so there are no groups to go to – I know, how dare they! This may sound like not such a bad thing but it is very much a bad thing when you have a baby that needs plastic shit to play with and other babies to swap germs with. Off you trot to your other usual hang outs – the park, the cafe, the museum, only to find that they are full of other people's children during school holidays – eek! These school age children are ruining all your favourite baby hang outs by being bigger and noisier and, Oh God, look at that queue! Suddenly six weeks seems like a long time.

When we moved north, the summer holidays were the real killer for me. I had met lots of people and chatted to them at groups but I didn't have any real friends to relax with. I was bored and lonely and that first summer was a real drag. By the next year, I'd got to know people a little more and had playdates and people to talk to and it felt better, but by the third summer I was so busy I never really got to catch up with half of the people I wanted to. It took a good three years to go from not having enough friends to fill the holidays to not having enough holiday for all my friends.

5. Being near family is brilliant. There were two reasons we moved to Yorkshire. The obvious reason, and the one I am contractually obliged to recite as a Yorkshire woman, is that it's the best place in the world to live. But, in reality, there were two very different reasons. Grandma- and Grandad-shaped reasons.

Small children look at grandparents and see biscuits and cuddles and fun. Parents look at grandparents and see a night out drinking and if you're super lucky a lie in. We are super lucky, our children have sleepovers at Grandma's.

If you move to be nearer babysitters, you can end up in the bizarre situation where you now have babysitters but also nowhere to go. I mean clearly there are plenty of places to go but until you have a network of friends you're stuck with each other. Which is lovely, obviously, it's not in the least bit depressing going out for dinner with your partner after spending months and months at home together. No darling

I'm really looking forwards to 'date night' maybe you could tell me again about the guy you sit next to at work who keeps farting and I can fill you in with tales of the week's best tantrums all over again but this time over candlelight and a pizza. Delightful.

Relocating to be nearer family who can help out with childcare is brilliant. It's fantastic to see how close my children are with their grandparents. In fact, without their support you would not be reading this book because I wouldn't have anything funny to say, I'd be too busy crying.

6. Being a parent is challenging wherever you live. I started writing a blog thinking it would be full of the differences between being a mum in London and being a mum in Yorkshire. But guess what? There are no differences. Being a mum is the same wherever you choose to live. Our lives are different but the day-to-day looking after children is no harder or easier.

The only real difference was the songs at playgroup. In London we were used to singing traditional children's songs from Africa, Mexico and Germany. In Yorkshire, all the songs are about farming. My daughter's requests for *Savez-Vous Plantez les Choux?* were met with blank looks, even though technically that is a song about growing cabbages.

Sometimes I miss my life in London but then I realise what I'm actually nostalgic for is life before children. Then someone starts screaming for a biscuit and I realise I wouldn't want to change a single thing about my life as it is now. Except maybe the screaming. Our lives are radically different from when we lived in a city but that has a lot to do with having children and less to do with where we live.

7. Nice places to live still cost money. We all do it, that fantasising in the back of our minds where we move somewhere quieter and buy a huge pile for next to nothing. House prices must be lower in Yorkshire... how much do you reckon we could get Downton Abbey for? And then you start looking and realise that actually all the places you would want to live still cost actual money. If a town has a good selection of places to work, nice fields full of sheep, and a busy high street – chances are house prices are not going to be all that cheap.

Also, this time you have to factor school catchment areas into your house search. Thinking about schools when your children are not even walking can be daunting – try not to get too stressed out by it. Save that particular panic for a later date when you have a three-year-old, and mass hysteria breaks out at playgroup.

Does any of this help? Probably not, although one way of thinking is this… at least when you do relocate you can stop *talking* about whether or not to relocate (which was frankly boring the arse off me by that point). The best thing about relocating our family was that once we'd made the leap, we no longer had to have lengthy discussions about it. Now we just sit in our slightly larger home and look at sheep.

Chapter 15
The loneliness of the long-serving mother

Only boring people get bored. Which is true but then you've just had a baby so you are officially a boring person, because becoming a mother is not the time to start being exciting. Peeling down to your sexy underwear on a naughty weekend break before drunkenly deciding 'Let's make a baby!' *is* exciting. It was being exciting that got you into this mess. Being boring might be tedious but it rarely ends in childbirth.

The biggest irony of parenting is that, at a time when you are never alone, you can often feel quite lonely. Being lonely is a big part of being a mum. If you add the worry that everyone else is doing a better job than you – that's pretty much the whole first three years of parenting. There are things you can do to counteract the loneliness of motherhood, basically they all involve finding other people to talk to. Making friends is the key to survival, having someone to hang out with can make the day fly by instead of dragging on. And if you actually like that person that's even better! Here are a few ideas.

1. Make friends whenever you have the chance. Lots of friends, too many friends, make friends with people you have lots in common with, make friends with people you have nothing in common with, make friends who annoy you a little bit, make friends with people you don't really like at all. Swipe right, swipe right, swipe right again.

It all boils down to this: on a rainy November afternoon do you want to sit in and listen to your baby crying or would you rather be in someone else's front room drinking coffee and being annoyed by every single thing they say? Maybe you'll pick the staying at home alone option... but at least you'll have that choice.

2. Do things you wouldn't normally do. I'm not thinking hula hooping through town naked although that definitely falls into the not boring category. I'm talking about more mundane stuff, the stuff you would never have dreamed of doing before you had a baby. Where once my evenings were filled with nights out, post baby my social life became: *The Great British Bake Off.* And I don't even like baking.

So I did some things I wouldn't have dreamed of doing before I had kids: I joined the Pre School Committee, an all-girls MMA/ Kickboxing class, The W.I. (no laughing at the back) and I Morris danced seven miles over a bloody great hill for charity.

Hear me out on the committee: I know it's all a bit Charlotte from *Sex And The City* and you're more of a Carrie/ Miranda hybrid with the occasional dash of Samantha but committees are great fun! Honestly, stick with me. They involve meetings where you talk about stuff that has *nothing* to do with sleep routines, teething or cracked nipples, sometimes there is wine (who am I kidding – there's always wine at ours) plus it means getting out of bedtime at home.

See, told you! Never has contributing to society looked so appealing!

The kickboxing I mistakenly signed up for whilst drunk at a New Year's Eve party, but three years on and I LOVE it. Kicking and punching is the best way to end or start a day with small children, it's got everything – exercise, stress relief, and other people to talk to. We even have a Christmas party which is fabulous because when you're at home with a baby the Christmas party invites are thin on the ground.

As for the other two things, my partner is still convinced I'm joking every time I go to the W.I. and even bringing home a handmade decoupage Christmas bauble didn't persuade him I'm not actually having an affair. Let's just gloss over the whole Morris dancing episode, probably best forgotten.

3. Get Online. Social media is a double-edged sword; it can make you feel like crap but if you use it correctly it might just cheer you up. Facebook chat groups or texting sessions with friends are a great way to feel like you're still in contact with the real world, as long as it's not the only contact you have. I have a group of mum friends on Facebook who all live in different parts of the country that I can chat with honestly about how I'm feeling, whether I'm angry, exhausted or depressed (I know, sounds like a right laugh!). It works brilliantly as a support network, and there is something empowering in knowing that while I'm sat in the loo hiding from another stressful teatime there's another mum doing exactly the same in Birmingham. Both of us can exchange sympathy wine emojis before tackling the spaghetti sauce on the ceiling together.

4. Meet ups. It's become more acceptable to admit that having a baby can be boring and, with that in mind, some rather fantastic ladies have organised meet ups, where mums with babies congregate in the local park and just hang out. If there is one near you, they are worth checking out. Maybe everyone there will be a massive twat and you'll hate it, but it's more likely that there'll be at least one mum who has the potential to be a lifelong friend.

If there isn't a meet up near you then take a deep breath and consider setting one up yourself. Let's face it, meeting a group of random strangers under a tree in the park will not be the most bonkers thing you ever do. Yesterday I left the house dressed as a 'space pirate' (my son's choice of outfit not mine).

5. The Mum Code: Pass It On. The stars of reality shows like *The Only Way Is Essex* and *Made in Chelsea* always witter on about guy code and girl code and how you shouldn't drunkenly snog your best mate's ex but if you see your best friend snogging another best friend's ex you MUST tell them. Jesus, it's all so complicated. Why don't they just write the rules down and then people wouldn't keep making mistakes?

If you thought all that shit was behind you I've got some bad news. I'm setting up the mum code and I'm writing it down. Once you've built up your network of friends, and have people to hang out with, it's your duty to keep an eye out for other mums. I don't expect you to flag down everybody with a pram and start chatting with them but just to remember how lonely motherhood can be and when that nervous-looking mum walks into playgroup or the park for the first time try to make her welcome. Say hello. It's always easier to start up a conversation when you're in a group and the good news is every time you do this the Gods of good fortune will smile down upon you and the next time your baby has a terrible bottom explosion it'll be on Daddy's watch not yours.

Chapter 16
Let's do this all over again...

For me there was no decision to be made because something, somewhere, deep down inside me wanted to have two babies... so that's what I did. I should have realised what I was in for when I was pregnant and looking after a toddler. I was exhausted, and grumpy and everything was shit. The last time I'd been pregnant it was all about me, people were running around after me, offering me seats, making me cups of tea, telling me to go home and have a sleep. Me, me, big fat puffy-footed, constipated me.

Second time round it's all about the baby you already have and that baby doesn't give a shit about you being pregnant. Your baby doesn't care if you're tired or feeling sick or need to put your ugly, puffy feet up before your toes explode like sausages in a frying pan. They want you to roll around on the floor and rescue the bit of puzzle that has rolled under the sofa and then they roll it straight back under because it was so much fun watching you roll around on the floor like an upturned turtle. Where once your old work colleagues would offer to make you endless cups of herbal tea or pop out and grab your lunch so they can avoid finishing spreadsheets, at home with a baby no one has boring work tasks they want to avoid. Instead, your older child sits waiting for your bump to grow big enough to use as a place to sit. Make the most of all the attention during your first pregnancy because second time around is too late. I am in awe of women who have three or more children; they are clearly bonkers in the most brilliant way... and tired, oh so tired.

If pregnancy second time around is tough, there is some good news about having a second baby – you get another shot at childbirth! This time everything will be marvellous!

And it was.

I mean it still hurt but the whole 'what the fuck is going to happen here?' business is dealt with because you have some idea of what you are in for. For me, I was less scared, my partner was less annoying and the whole thing was quicker. Let's face it, if you could change anything about childbirth, surely making it quicker, less annoying and not so terrifying would be a pretty good place to start. For me, giving birth second time around, I felt like I almost knew what I was doing. In fact, I'd go so far as to say that next time I'd definitely nail it. If I ever did have another baby which is almost definitely, probably not going to happen, I think.

Keen to maintain the level of panic as new parents, we decided to start worrying about how our first child would react to having a new baby around. Would she feel left out? Would she be upset? How could we introduce the new baby to her life without causing a massive upheaval? People out there have cottoned onto this new parent panic and have handily produced all kinds of story books about having a new sibling, with lovely pictures and cute explanations about how Mummy and Daddy will still love them even though there's another baby in the house. People worry about explaining difficult concepts to small children – like the time we took our daughter to a lesbian wedding. The only thing she found the slightest bit out of the ordinary was that the hotel we stayed in had a kettle in the bedroom, which when you think about it is a weird idea. Why would you boil water in your bedroom? It makes absolutely no sense. The rest of the day was simple, Aunty Laura loves Aunty Rachel so they're getting married. End of. Same with the new baby. One day Mummy had a big tummy, the next day there was a baby to play with, that was that, we could have skipped the dull books about Mummy laying an egg and stuck with reading the same book about a rabbit that goes skating that we had to read every night for a whole three years. Not sure which was worse.

When my son was born we were ready for the new baby love bubble but we assumed it would be on a lesser scale second time around. Not that we'd love baby number two less but that we'd have more of a handle on our emotions. And then we had him and we were totally floored. Exactly like first time around, like being hit by a train all over again. In fact, I loved him so much I genuinely thought there might actually be something wrong with me. I still worry about this now, at three years old he is showered with kisses daily because he is my youngest and my baby. The thought that one day he will not want me snuggling him to death at every opportunity makes me want to burst into tears.

For the first six months, life was perfect with our perfect baby and a perfect toddler, for starters I wasn't pregnant anymore *and* I sort of knew what I was doing, all the fear from first time around had vanished and we enjoyed looking after a new-born. Turns out having babies is amazing fun if you can cut out all the worrying. If I'm honest, at first our lives hardly changed; obviously we were totally smitten and chuffed to bits to have another person in our family but other than that he had little to no impact on our lives. Everything was going so well. Breastfeeding was easier second time around, we were more prepared for the sleep deprivation and some of the fear about dropping the baby and breaking it had gone. In fact he did get dropped, I left him snoozing for a few seconds and returned to find him sprawled on the floor after his sister had dragged him out of the pram by his feet. I know if that had happened with our first born I would have been traumatised, but second time around it simply made for a funny story, because, hey, we were cool man, we'd chilled out and we had the hang of this parenting lark. When people asked me 'What's it like having two young children at 40?' I chirpily replied 'Not so bad'. I'd go so far as to say we were pretty smug about our decision. What a fool I was. Remember the mantra: this too shall pass. Never imagine you are in control. The moment you pretend to know what you are doing, things will fall to shit.

When our son was six months old, we chucked all our belongings in storage and flew to the States for a fun-packed six weeks. We got caught up in a hurricane in New York when our flights out were cancelled and all the trains shut down. Watching the 24-hour news reports predicting the end of the world and seeing the empty grocery store shelves, we decided to make a dash for it, driving down deserted highways with the radio tuned to emergency services broadcasting so we would know if we had to get off the road. We did this with a toddler, a baby and one packet of cookies. At about the same time, our perfect baby son woke up and started to have what I can only describe as: opinions. He continues to have opinions to this day. Mainly his opinion is that he disagrees strongly with what is happening and he likes to throw himself on the floor in anguish and cry. He had very strong opinions for an entire flight from Boston to San Francisco and he voiced them so forcefully other passengers on the plane didn't even look annoyed they all just smiled pityingly at us.

After six months of barely registering he was there, one day the boy woke up and got annoyed and never really stopped being annoyed. Whereas our daughter was always on an even keel, our son ricocheted from massive belly laughs to complete distress. It was as though we'd had a second baby and this second baby was a *totally different person* to the other child we already had. Who knew that would happen? It turns out babies are just like actual people and brothers and sisters can all be wildly different!

At nine months, my son was up and walking, in totally different directions to his two-year-old sister, the pair of them running into walls, doors and table legs. By the time I'd rescued one from climbing over the stair gate (at the top of the stairs) the other one had got stuck in a kitchen cupboard. It was knackering, not quite new baby knackered (the pinnacle of knackered) or pregnant knackered (a special uber level of exhaustion reserved solely for the female sex) but looking-after-two-children-moving-in-different-directions-knackered comes in a close third.

Living with an adventurous baby and a two-year-old with no sense of danger was like starring in a daily episode of *Jackass*, but in our preschool version of the show, instead of high fiving each other and saying "Dude that was sweeeeet," after each stunt it was just me running around the house all tense and sweaty, shouting "Put that down NOW!" and "How did you get up there?"

I once met a mum at the library who asserted that she would not be putting up stair gates as "children have an innate sense of fear" which would stop them from falling down the stairs. I never saw her again, I can only presume she was busy ferrying her family to and from the hospital on a daily basis. Children do not have an innate sense of fear, they are attracted to danger. When my daughter was two, she invented a fun game which involved covering her own eyes, assuming she was invisible and walking into lamp posts.

There was a period of about six months when we really struggled with having two children pulling in two different directions. In fact, a little bit of us wondered if we hadn't made a bit of a mistake. All around me, my friends with babies were getting into the fun bit with their babies walking and talking, while I was too busy running out of cafes in floods of tears because I couldn't handle the embarrassment of another public tantrum. Really, truly, honestly as much as we loved the very bones of him sometimes it was difficult not to look at people with one baby and think how much more fun we'd be having with just one child to look after.

The phrase you will hear on constant repeat is: It will be lovely when they're a bit older and they can play together. Fast forward a couple of years and my children are now a bit older and holy shit they do play together! They were right! It is lovely. Noisy and argumentative but very, very lovely. Even if we don't always share the same opinion on important things like how often you should wear pants (every day, yes, even on a weekend) and how many biscuits you can eat for breakfast (none).

The other annoying phrase you will always hear is 'Make the most of it, while they're young, they grow up so fast!' which implies that the baby phase is over before you know it. Which it is when you're out of the other side of it, but when you're slap, bang, in the middle and your mate with older children tells you her kids didn't sleep through til they were about three or four? Aaargh! Time does not fly when you're up three times a night.

Babies and small children are wonderful but they are also quite annoying and sometimes infuriating. It's okay to admit this, it doesn't mean you love your children any less it just means you are being honest about what is involved with being a parent. Some ages are harder than others, in fact some children are more difficult than others. I thought I was doing a great job when I just had my daughter – turns out it was nothing to do with my parenting skills she was just quite well-behaved! My son was another matter completely but after three years of tantrums we have learned to see the funny side and accept that not everything is within our control. Children have their own, tiny, crazy ideas and sometimes whatever you do is not good enough so you just have to sit down in the park, pull out your smartphone and wait for a three-year-old to stop screaming in the bushes because he doesn't want to wear shoes anymore. When you spot that mum ignoring a crying child and checking Facebook, don't look down your nose, give her a little smile instead, just in case you ever find yourself trying to extricate a shoeless toddler from a shrubbery yourself.

Know that there are some days when being a parent requires you to sit on the toilet, binge-eating Jaffa Cakes and crying. Everyone has a turn at this, even that woman that you see at playgroup sometimes who wears white jeans and has blow-dried hair. Anytime you see a mum who looks like she's doing better than you, remember that it's not a competition, and if it was you'd be winning because who else is a better mum to your baby than you?

Appendix
Five-of-the-Best
Blog Posts

How to survive playgroup

If the idea of walking into a room full of angry babies, exhausted mums and germ-ridden toys fills you with dread then know that you are not alone.

The whole idea terrified me and I've performed stand-up comedy.

Playgroups can be noisy, intimidating places and as the responsible adult it is generally considered unacceptable to burst into tears and throw yourself on the floor screaming if you decide you don't really like it.

But playgroups are worth the effort. In time, you will learn to love them, so much so that by the time July comes round you'll be horrified at the thought of going cold turkey over the summer holidays.

We do at least 3 playgroups a week - as we have recently moved I don't even have friends to gossip with. I have been to groups in London and Yorkshire and there are essentially no differences between the two (Yorkshire playgroups feature more songs about farm animals and tractors).

If you do decide you hate playgroup it's always worth trying another to see if it suits you better: I once went to a playgroup where I was the oldest mum there.

By 20 years.

I go because my children love playgroups and I love my children.

I go because I see how much they learn being surrounded by other children.

I go because if I stayed at home with a 2 year old and a 1 year old every day I would lose my shit.

Here are the 10 things you should know about playgroup.

1. There will be tea and coffee.

It will be awful.

It will also often be served in cups and saucers. Like an evil round of *Total Wipeout*, sleep deprived adults are challenged to carry scalding hot drinks through a room packed with toy cars and manic children.

If you want good coffee, go to Caffe Nero. Entertain your own children.

2. There will be toys.

Lots of them.

Take a moment to look around the room and marvel at all its hideous plastic glory. Thank the Lord that none of these toys are cluttering up your own home.

There will be one toy that will cause 98% of all trouble.

Every single child will want to play with this one toy. It will probably be a pram, a slide or a ride on car. This is the law of the playgroup: The more toys there are in a room the more children will be attracted to just one toy.

3. There will be germs.

Everywhere.

You will catch colds, coughs, sneezes, tummy bugs, slap cheek, foot and mouth, and anything else that is going.

Sorry.

The other option is isolating your child from all contact with other children and letting them catch everything when they start school. The decision is yours.

4. There will be painting or crafts.

Just as Grandma's house is the ideal place for small children to bake, playgroup is the perfect spot for painting and crafts. Remember to admire whatever crappy effort your child produces and try not to be caught stuffing it in the bin outside the church door.

5. There will be one child sitting quietly doing puzzles.

This will not be your child.

I had hoped this role was allocated on some sort of rota and that one week it would be my daughter quietly amusing herself whilst others looked on in awe. I seem to have been left off the rota.

(If I had a child who sat quietly and entertained themselves I would not need playgroup. I would be sitting at home watching This Morning, painting my toenails and writing a blog about what a piece of piss small children are to look after.)

6. There will be one single male.

He will look totally out of his depth.

His partner will either be heavily pregnant or have recently given birth. Basically the situation at home is so terrifying he has decided playgroup is the better option.

Women go to playgroup because they want to get out of the house, men are sent to playgroup by women who want to get them out of the house.

7. There will be well meaning volunteers.

They will either be brilliant with small children or totally ineffectual. Who cares? They have volunteered to spend a morning picking wooden bricks up off the floor that your children have thrown. They are wonderful, misguided people.

8. There will be snack.

To work out what type of snack simply look inside the cavity of any toy where you will find a handy guide in the form of a half-eaten snack from last week.

9. There will be singing.

It will be awful.

A platoon of Gareth Malone's could not make a playgroup singing session sound good.

You will sing Sleeping Bunnies. Twice. Despite the fact that it is a song with no discernible tune.

You will sing Row, Row, Row Your Boat and learn some dubious wildlife survival tips.

You will sing a sexist, outdated version of The Wheels On The Bus. (Altogether now: The Mummy's on the bus read Gra – Zi – Ah.)

10. There will be tidying up.

It will be wonderful.

If tidying up at home involved throwing everything in a plastic box and hiding it in a cupboard, my life would be improved immeasurably.

So there you are... playgroup for beginners.

How to visit friends with small children: 10 things you need to know

I get it, you're just not that that into kids. Thing is your friends have acquired some and now you're forced to spend time with them.

You've hung out together when they were babies and that wasn't too bad but now they're walking and talking and doing, er, whatever it is they do.

When you don't have any of your own to practice on, hanging out with other people's children can be a bit scary.

Fear not.

This guide features everything you need to know about kidlets but couldn't be arsed to ask.

1. Children are fucking stupid.

Ignore parents who waffle on about how clever their kids are.

They're sleep deprived and talking bollocks.

Imagine a big stupid dog, full of energy, bouncing all over the place.

Yeah, well my kids are even more stupid than that dog. At least you can lock the dog outside overnight.

My two-year-old son still doesn't know how to use a straw properly.

A straw for fuck's sake.

Move your hot drinks out of reach and don't give them anything with a pointy end.

Once you've got your head round this, everything else makes sense.

2. Let them come to you.

So your best friend is now a mum/dad and you're ready to be the coolest uncle/aunt on the block.

Unfortunately, children don't give a shit about the fact that you once saved Daddy from choking on his own vomit on a stag do.

So don't try too hard.

Children don't like adults who try to give them cuddles as soon as they walk in the room.

The more eager you are, the more they will run away from you.

Conversely if you want to stay as far away as possible from them, ignoring children is a big mistake.

My children have a built-in homing device for people who want to avoid children.

The grumpy man in the cafe? Ker-ching!

That couple arguing on the train? Ba-doom!

So basically, don't give them too much attention but don't ignore them either.

It's a tricky thing to master but totally worth it in the end.

Maybe.

Your friends' kids could be dicks for all I know.

3. Buying gifts is a minefield.

You know how hil-ar-ious you think it will be to buy a toddler a plastic trumpet?

Well it won't be. It will be funny for precisely 7 minutes.

Then there will be tears.

Many, many tears as the trumpet is forcibly removed and hidden in the bin.

Followed by a weird atmosphere and questions about the time of your train home.

Try not to take offence if the special present you spent ages choosing is tossed immediately to one side.

Of all the beautiful gifts from close friends and family, my daughter became attached to a plastic phone that was free with a CBeebies magazine.

Best to explain that honestly you have no idea what children like, so you brought wine instead.

Lots of lovely wine.

4. Children love repetition.

This is a good thing because it means, as a visitor, you only need one 'trick' to keep them entertained, for example: hiding a toy or pretend biting their toes.

It is also a bad thing because small children have the endurance of an ultra marathon runner.

They will literally NEVER tire of you hiding that rabbit.

Even when you are diagnosed with repetitive strain injury.

Don't worry if it all ends in tears.

5. Everything ends in tears.

Small children cry all the time, over anything.

Because they are tired, because they are two, because they want the green plate but they don't know what the colour green looks like, so actually they really want the yellow plate which is in fact not a plate at all but a fucking cup.

Seriously how the hell is anyone supposed to know this shit?!

There is literally NO way to avoid tears.

Give them the red plate and don't worry if it makes them cry.

6. Children can be magnificently rude.

Try to think of the worst thing anyone could ever say to you.

Then imagine someone shouting it loudly into your face in public.

Wait for the best bit!

You are supposed to laugh it off like it's all a big funny joke.

And you can't even call bullshit when the red-faced parents tell you little Bobby doesn't really understand what fat/ugly means yet.

Yes, he does. And he thinks you're it.

Whilst it is unacceptable to punch a small child in the face it is okay to think about it.

7. Never say 'Should you be doing that?'

No they should not.

But they are.

And now it's up to you as a responsible adult to stop them.

In this situation, the best course of action as a visitor is to back out of the room quickly and pretend you haven't seen them doing whatever they should not be doing.

Oh and it's polite to offer to cook while parents do an emergency dash to the hospital.

8. Don't ask parents to translate.

We don't know what they're saying either.

If someone speaks a foreign language. you can usually guess what they mean by identifying a few key phrases.

This does not work for toddlers.

My son's identifiable keywords are usually dinosaur, helicopter, biscuit.

I have NEVER seen a stegosaurus flying in emergency custard creams.

I have, however, developed a foolproof system for creating the illusion that I understand what small children are saying.

I call it the three R's; every time they speak to you deploy one of these handy options.

React: Say 'Oh No! That's scary/ big/amazing!'

Reassure: Reply 'Well done!/ That's okay/ Not to worry'

Reward: Give them a biscuit.

Using my system, anyone can at least look like they know what they're doing.

9. Early evenings are hell.

Photographers call the early evening hours – the magic hour or golden hour.

Parents call it something else.

The hours before bed are the noisiest, most distressing time of the day.

It's when everyone in the family spits out their last bit of anger and upset.

If you are staying overnight, this is probably a good time to check out the local pub.

If there is no pub, sitting outside in the garden wondering how on earth the neighbours have never called the police is acceptable.

10. It is okay to blame the children.

For bad smells or breakages or the fact that you and your best mate from college now have literally nothing in common.

It's not you, it's them.

Oh and remember when parents say *'They're not normally like this'* it could mean that they are usually worse.

Enjoy your weekend!

Do let me know how you get on.

Don't forget the wine.

Is my son a dick?

As a parent you quickly learn to interpret different screams – there's the tired scream, the I would like some attention scream and then there's the scream of your child in genuine pain. The one that turns your stomach. Thank God I have not had to hear that one very often from my daughter.

But my son does not follow these rules – he is the ultimate boy who cried wolf and will scream like a banshee for no apparent reason at all. He even does it in his sleep.

When you cannot find anything actually wrong with a crying baby, it is chalked up to the catch all excuse of teething. Teething is brilliant – I have been using it as an excuse for my general incompetence for some time now. So far I've used it as an explanation for forgotten birthdays, having a spotty chin, wearing odd socks, missed appointments and a general level of slovenliness around the house.

But I don't think my son cries because he is teething.

We only really have his sister to compare him with and she was a very different baby. A few people I've spoken to about this have said boys are more needy than girls. I'm really not a fan of blaming things on gender, it seems a bit harsh to tar the male population with one small child's bad temper.

The third excuse I've heard is that it is behaviour typical of a second child trying to get a parent's attention. But he's breastfed and I'm with him *all the time*. How much attention does he want?

I have come to the conclusion that there's a simple answer to his screaming fits.

My son is a dick.

Sorry to be so blunt but the writing has been on the wall for some time now. Eeh Bah Daughter's nickname is bubbles, Eeh Bah Son's only nickname is dick–douche (this has been adapted to DD after an unfortunate incident when his sister introduced him to prospective friends in the park).

His screaming doesn't affect how much we love him, he totally gets away with such behaviour as he is a super cute baby who caused minimal damage to my lady bits. My only hope is that he will grow out of it but I'd love to hear if anyone else thinks their offspring are dicks too.

Anyway must dash – I'm in the process of organising the kids bookshelf from least to most chewed. I'm calling it the Chewy Decimal System.

Sorry that was an awful joke, I couldn't help myself.

F*ckety F*ck... If he is a dick does he get it from me?

Things you will do as a parent you will not like

Once you have children you will find yourself doing lots of things that you said you would never do.

If you do not have children or plan on having children please feel free to enjoy this list with a smug aloofness (imagine you're a member of the Bullingdon Club) and when people tell you that you'll be missing out when you're older, remember it basically comes down to this:

We're all going to end up confused and needing help. Would you rather have your bum wiped by someone who hated you as a teenager or a complete stranger?

Here is my list of things I thought I would never do but ended up doing when I had them there children.

1. You will baby proof your home too soon then spend the next few months unable to get into your cupboards or up the stairs.

When babies are born they don't even realise that their hands belong to them.

They are therefore unlikely to stick fingers, which they don't know they have, into electrical wall sockets.

They are also highly unlikely to be opening the fridge or falling downstairs of their own accord whatever their older siblings may tell you.

This does not stop parents rushing to make their homes as safe as possible. What this really means is that your baby will grow up in an environment where there is a lot of swearing.

Those plastic plug socket protectors can only be removed with the blade of a knife and a liberal application of cursing.

The stair gates will become a dangerous trip hazard for sleep-deprived parents and the fridge lock will leave you unable to access any chilled food. (Top tip: Put a child lock on the cleaning cupboard and never clean again.)

By the time your baby does start to move around and explore the safety measures will have been removed in a cloud of foul language and you will only remember to put the stair gates back when you watch your beloved child bounce down the stairs head first.

2. You will sniff your baby's bum to check for poo.

I remember seeing parents doing this and thinking: Yuk that's disgusting. I am *never* doing that.

It is disgusting, and yes I have done it. Lots.

Even more disgusting is the reason why parents do this.

Let me spell this out as clearly as possible: Parents sniff baby's bums because they no longer have the mental capacity to detect the smell of shit even when they are sat right next to it.

Children are disgusting.

I blame the parents.

3. You will go out to eat and sit colouring in a picture of a man with a moustache making a pizza.

Because when you go out to eat with small children you are given colouring in kits. (I know, amazing!)

There are two reasons you as an adult will get stuck in:

Firstly, it is good fun to colour in a picture and you are fantastic at not going over the edges.

Secondly, you are too tired to have a conversation with the person sitting across the table from you. You have only left the house because neither of you has the energy to throw beans in a pan.

Think of this as me time. Who needs massages or spa days when you can spend 15 minutes in silence neatly filling in a cartoon of a pizza chef?

Even if it is quite challenging creating a realistic skin tone from four primary colours. Honestly how do they expect small children to manage?

(Top Tip: I carry my own skin tone crayon[7])

4. You will refer to your partner as Mummy or Daddy.

Even though all the books say you ABSOLUTELY MUST NOT do this because you and your partner will immediately stop fancying each other and you will never have sex ever again.

I wouldn't worry about it. There are many, many other things that will stop you from having sex – number one being the baby (total cock blocker).

Unless of course you are one of those people who likes sexy colouring in (Ooh, look, I've gone over the lines, naughty mummy).

In which case, having a baby is going to be a total game changer.

5. You will fantasize about the upstairs deck of a bus.

The top deck of a double decker bus will become like the VIP area of the nightclubs you used to frequent – a place of

---

[7] I absolutely do not do this but I have definitely thought about it.

mystery and intrigue, reserved for people whose lives are infinitely more exciting than yours.

But this is not the VIP area of some hot new club.

It is the top deck of a bus.

And you have a pram and cannot get in.

You have officially the most depressing life on the bus.

No wait... there's a man getting on at the next stop who is arguing with a copy of yesterday's Metro.

Phew, saved.

6. You will announce that you are a parent even when it is not relevant.

When you are not with your children you will feel the need to let people know that you have children stored somewhere else.

God forbid anyone should see you sitting there on the train and not realise that you have a baby at home.

'Can I take that seat?'

'Yes, I've got a 9-month-old baby at home.'

'Actually I'll stand.'

7. You will shout "Look Cow! Horse! Dog!" every time you see an animal.

You will do this even when there are no children with you.

It is a conditioned response, especially when you are in a car because this is when you are most desperate to entertain your children.

Travelling in a car with small children is like shaking a can full of soda, one small flick and it will all kick off and everyone nearby is getting a sticky face.

8. You will laugh at Michael McIntyre's jokes.

Just the stuff he does about being a parent.

You will either laugh because you find his parenting material funny (improbable) or because you are tired and grumpy and glad bad things are happening to Michael McIntyre (more likely).

9. You will reassess what constitutes soiled clothing.

You've been wearing that jumper all week but is it *actually* dirty?

Yes, yes it is. It is a dirty jumper.

Once you have a baby, the washing basket becomes less of a place to put washing in and more of a storage receptacle for clothes that are not quite dirty enough.

Vomit and poo stained clothes will forever be jumping the washing queue leaving clothes that are just plain old dirty in laundry basket limbo. Until you decide you need to change and then you will sort through your dirty clothes and refresh them with a baby wipe.[8]

10. You will drop your baby.

Or, even better smack it's head on the door frame in the middle of the night after spending hours rocking the little bugger to sleep.

Peaches Geldof was photographed talking on the phone whilst dropping her baby out of her pram.

It happens.

This, or something like this, will happen to you but the good news is there is unlikely to be any paparazzi on hand to catch your moment of shame.

Dropping your baby is not bad parenting it is just parenting.

If you have children and find things on this list you haven't done, please leave a comment and let the rest of us know how you managed it.

---

[8] This may just be me.

If you do not have children, yet, why not make your own list of things you do not intend on doing, pin it to the fridge and cross them off one by one as you watch all your principles vanish when the baby arrives.

What does your pram say about you?

Buying a pram is the most complicated adult process you can go through that doesn't require a solicitor.

Most parents buy their prams before baby arrives. If you've ever ordered lunch for someone who is late, you will know what a complicated decision making process that can be; when you are buying a pram you are essentially choosing something for a person who doesn't even exist yet.

Having said that, I doubt there is a mother alive who didn't know Kate Middleton would buy a Bugaboo. The go-to travel system for people with well-to-do grandparents, they are designed for 'busy urban lifestyles' and let's face it, if anyone is going to be hopping on and off a London bus it's the style conscious wife of the future King of England.

The Bugaboo is the pram equivalent of an LK Bennet nude court shoe.

Buying the pram is also the first time your partner shows any interest whatsoever in the baby you are about to have – it's the type of shopping Mr Eeh Bah likes to create a spreadsheet for (no joke).

So while your other half gets all Jeremy Clarkson (I mean in a vehicle reviewing sense not punching Piers Morgan or insulting Mexicans) here are the questions most mums-to-be will want answering.

How do I look pushing the pram?

Go on try it… Yeah, you'll look great cruising down the high street off to grab a coffee.

Now try pushing the pram with one hand whilst holding a hot beverage in the other hand. Can you still steer?

Great! You're a natural... Damn, now the phone is ringing.

Try holding the pram steady with your leg – there is a brake but it will not really work very well... oh and you're wearing flip flops, you cannot apply a pram brake wearing flip flops – FACT.

Anyway concentrate – with your lower body, stop your beloved child from rolling off into oncoming traffic, hold hot drink in one hand, and answer your phone before... no missed it.

It's your partner, call him back, (try hitting buttons with your chin). He is 'just phoning to check you are alright?'

You are not alright. You are trying to stop your most treasured possession (the baby not the pram) from rolling into a busy road whilst drinking coffee (stick to soft drinks in future) and shouting swearwords into the phone.

So how *do* you look pushing the pram?

You look like someone people would cross the street to avoid.

In short, you look like a new mum. So go ahead buy the yellow umbrella or the grey one, who gives a toss.

Which way should baby be facing?

For those of you out of the loop, the big development in pushchairs is that they are nearly all now parent facing. Basically, it means that when you are at your wit's end with the baby crying in the house, you can leave home and still have a baby screaming in your face.

Isn't modern design wonderful? God forbid that you and your baby should go out for a relaxing stroll and look at trees or dogs or other people enjoying themselves without children. No, there must be direct line of sight between you and your baby at all times.

I used an old non-parent facing pram which was cheap/free, and was lovingly nicknamed The Beast.

The downside of the outward facing pram is that you have to decipher what your child is doing by reading the looks on people's faces as they walk towards you.

Here is a quick guide:

Smiles or comments about how cute your child is = Baby is asleep.

Pitying looks = Baby is crying.

Looks of horror = Baby is covered in vomit or the wind has stuck a crisp packet to its face.

What does this pram say about me as a mother?

For example, a Stokke pram looks like you are wheeling a bar stool around the streets and allows your baby to sit up high. It says, 'I am design conscious and my house is full of expensive things that this child will ruin' – and my baby is staring directly in your face, look at my baby, LOOK AT IT.

Do not buy this pram if there is the slightest chance your baby will be ugly.

If this were a shoe, it would be a Nicholas Kirkwood or Charlotte Olympia showstopper.

A three wheeler says 'I am sporty and health conscious and I walk everywhere and shop at farmers markets' – mainly because I cannot get my pram on the bus or through the door of any high street shops.

These prams are heavy. I wouldn't be surprised if Jessica Ennis is not pushing a Phil & Ted's as part of her training regime.

They are the shoe equivalent of a pair of Birkenstocks (not the fancy fur lined Celine ones).

And, of course, then there is the Maclaren that you will end up buying in the end anyway.

It's the push chair that laughs in the face of all the other fancy travel systems.

As far as footwear goes, the Maclaren is an old pair of Converse – while all the other shoes are at home gossiping in the bottom of the wardrobe these are out doing all the work.

But which one did you choose?

Other Books from Bennion Kearny

I've Got a Stat For You: My Life With Autism

by Andrew Edwards

At the age of four, Andrew Edwards was diagnosed with autism. "Go home and watch Rain Man," the specialist told his mother. "In all probability your son will be institutionalised." Determined to prove the specialist wrong, Andrew's mother set out to give her son the best life possible.

I've got a Stat for You is an honest and compelling account of one young man's journey to manage his autism and achieve his goals. Raised in a single parent household and encountering bureaucracy, bullying, and a lack of understanding from many around him, Andrew emerged from a turbulent childhood to win a Welsh National Young Volunteer Award, give speeches on his condition, and secure his dream job as a statistician at Manchester United Television.

From Wrexham to Buckingham Palace, and incorporating stories of The Simpsons, sport, music, and strange smells – *I've got a Stat for You* is a powerful and inspirational tale that shows how determination, a positive outlook, and the will to succeed can overcome all odds!

How to Help Your Teenager Achieve Exam Success: A Parent's Guide

by April Miller

"Children must be taught how to think, not what to think." Margaret Mead

Achievement in any sphere does not happen accidentally, it usually requires hard work, sustained effort and effective strategies. Exam success is no different.

Written by an experienced A-Level teacher, this up-to-date, accessible – but most importantly concise - book offers practical advice for parents on how best to help their teenagers achieve exam success.

Based on her time in the teaching profession and a wide number of educational studies, April Miller offers achievable and evidence-based advice on how to help your teenager fulfil their potential.

As you read this book, you will learn how your teenager thinks and how to help them think in an academically successful way. Their thinking patterns are not the same as adults!